MW01258233

ENDORSEMENT ... RICHARD BRIGHT

"For good or for bad, every dad has the power to change the world for his kids. There is no heavier baggage than what comes from an absent or unhealthy father.

There's no greater blessing than the blessing that comes from a loving Dad. For every man who wants to a healthy dad, this book is for you!

Other than God Himself, there are no perfect fathers, but despite all our imperfections, God gives us the grace to be good dads if we're willing to make the effort.

This book is a roadmap to help you discover inner healing for your own "dad wounds" so that you can be the man and the father God created you to be. The four men who wrote this book are the real deal. As you read their stories, you'll laugh, you might shed a few tears and you'll also be inspired to look at fatherhood in a new way.

Every man needs this book. I'm so thankful for this message. This book will change the world if dads will read it and apply its message."

*-Dave Willis, Father of four sons, pastor, and Author of "Think Like Jesus"*

---

I talk to so many people who struggle with their relationship with God because they project the face of their earthly father onto their Heavenly Father.

This book is a great way to start the journey of healing the wounds from our earthly father and seeing God for the perfect father that he is.

*Joël Malm, Founder of Summit Leaders and Author of Love Slows Down*

Being a dad is one of the hardest jobs you will ever have as a man. It's important to watch and talk to dad's that are farther along the journey than you. For me, one of those men that I look up to is Richard Bright. He is an amazing husband, father, pastor, and friend. He isn't a perfect dad, but over the years I've watched how he does his best to emulate his heavenly Father when dealing with his children. Richard is a man on a mission with a desire to help other men recognize the love that is available through the Perfect Father.

*Imperfect Dads, One Perfect Father* is such a valuable resource that all men need in their lives. We all have dads that did their best, but we all have a Heavenly Father longing to restore areas of our lives that need attention. You need to buy a copy for yourself, and for the men in your life, so they can receive the love and adoration from their Perfect Father.

*Clayton Hurst | Marriage Pastor*
*Lakewood Church – Houston, TX*

# ENDORSEMENT FOR GEORGE GREGORY

Just like a diamond has its own imperfections we call flaws, so do we as men. George provides clarity to assist men on how to navigate the role of being a friend, a son, a brother, and a father. As each of those roles changes due to time and environments, George uses insight from personal experiences on how to make the adjustments to stay true to one's own self while growing as a man. There is a brilliance in each of us, and George has a way of showing men how to shine.

*Arthur J. Hightower II*
*Senior Director of Player Engagement*
*Los Ángeles Chargers*

---

I am extremely grateful for the endless love, mentorship, and support of my father throughout the years. As a son, his stories and examples have help me navigate life's challenges on my journey to manhood. He has given me the greatest gift I could have ever asked for - he believed in me. It is through that belief that I now am able to live my dreams. I highly recommend this book for fathers of all ages to glean insights and wisdom for your journey.

*Jaylen Gregory (son of George Gregory),*
*Environmental Scientist at Stantec*

---

For several years I've had the honor of calling George Gregory my friend as we have walked through different challenges in our lives. He is a man of integrity, a devoted husband, loving father, and a pastor to many. Whether he is speaking in front of thousands or just to you face to face, there is no one like George! He will be your fiercest supporter, constant encourager, and loudest cheerleader as you journey through life.

Through his many speaking engagements or numerous books, George is someone you want speaking into your life! I am just one of many that continues to be impacted by his life and ministry!

*Clayton Hurst, Marriage Pastor*
*Lakewood Church*
*Houston, Tx*

# ENDORSEMENT FOR JUAN MARTINEZ

Beyond the yellow brick road is one jewel of wisdom you must add to the treasure box. Every opposition we face in life is just another opportunity to display to those around us that we have promises that can be trusted from a God who cares about every detail of our lives. Pastor Juan Martinez truly describes the heartbeat of the father and points everyone into the direction that heals and restores - Jesus Christ

*Bryann Trejo*
*Kingdom Muzic overseer minister of music*

---

"Jesus tells us those who have been forgiven much, love much. With a divine love like Juan Martinez has for people, you have to understand there's a backstory that brought him to this place. Pastor Juan has lived the highs and lows of life and has come out broken and with a limp but as a man that you know has been with God.

His insights of a deep relational walk with God will help everybody young and old make the most of their journey and their story. I'm thankful for Pastor Juan taking the time to share these deep, accessible truths to help the Body of Christ walk in a deeper relationship with Jesus!"

*Mike Rosas*
*UpRising Society and Chaplain of the Houston Rockets*

---

I have experienced first hand how God can change anyone. What started as a friendship, then lead to Mentorship, and now a spiritual parent to me Pastor Juan has not only been with me through my whole journey but has helped pave my own Yellow Brick Road. Juan's passion for Christ not only oozes out of his body but countless souls have witnessed God's hand through his powerful ministry. Beyond the Yellow Brick Road will not only give you insight to Juan's unique revelations but most of all will expose you to the Love of Jesus Christ. His transparency and ability to share the gospel can relate to those struggling but will also give great hope that there is another way out. Enjoy!

*Vinny DeLeon*
*Pastor - Get Wrapped Church*
*Owner- Vinny's Barbershop*

# ENDORSEMENT FOR SCOTT SILVERII

Daddy. I love you Daddy. You are my Daddy.

*Max Silverii (my son)*
*15 years old. Blessed by Down syndrome.*

---

Scott is one of the most humble, gracious, & authentic men I've ever known. He's the example of what every one of us is called to be as a Godly man, husband, & father. Scott is the real deal & is helping change the lives & legacies of fathers now & for generations to come.

*John Finch*
*Storyteller of The Father Effect Book & Movie*

# IMPERFECT DADS, ONE PERFECT FATHER

ENCOURAGING MEN THROUGH THE JOURNEY OF
FATHERHOOD

RICHARD BRIGHT    GEORGE GREGORY
JUAN MARTINEZ    SCOTT SILVERII

# COPYRIGHT

© 2021 *Five Stones Press*

*All rights reserved. No part of this publication may be reproduced, distributed, or transmitted in any form or by any means, including photocopying, recording, or other electronic or mechanical methods, without the prior written permission of the publisher, except in the case of brief quotations embodied in critical reviews and certain other noncommercial uses permitted by copyright law. For permission requests, contact Five Stones Press.*

All Scripture quotations, unless otherwise indicated, are taken from the New American Standard Bible, ©1960, 1962, 1963, 1968, 1971, 1972, 1973, 1975, 1977, 1995 by The Lockman Foundation. Used by permission.

Other versions used are:

KJV—King James Version. Authorized King James Version.

NIV—Scripture taken from the Holy Bible, New International Version®. Copyright © 1973, 1978, 1984 by International Bible Society. Used by permission of Zondervan Publishing House. All rights reserved.

First Edition

Cover Design: Wicked Smart Designs

Editorial Team: Kimberly Cannon & Ava Hodge

Interior Formatting: Five Stones Press Design Team

Publisher: Five Stones Press, Dallas, Texas

www.fivestonespress.org

For quantity sales, textbooks, and orders by trade bookstores or wholesalers contact Five Stones Press at publish@fivestonespress.net

Five Stones Press is owned and operated by Five Stones Church, a nonprofit 501c3 religious organization. Press name and logo are trademarked. Contact publisher for use.

Printed in the United States of America

# DEDICATION

*Richard, George, Juan and Scott dedicate this book to you, Dad. You were created by God the perfect Father to be an incredible dad. We have prayed over you and your commitment to walk through this book with the faith that God speaks to you and affirms you as father.*

# CONTENTS

# INTRODUCTION

"Daddy."

What a wonderful word to hear. Daddy is also an incredible word to say. So many men have been blessed with a loving, nurturing relationship with their dad, and what an incredible blessing this relationship is to father and child.

Another wonderful experience is becoming a dad and enjoying an exceedingly close and loving connection with your own child. But the reality is, not every man who has children has heard that loving word "Daddy," nor have all men been able to speak that word to their own father. It can become a complex relationship, but it can indeed become a story of reconciliation and restoration.

All four of us guys who came together to write this book are dads. We've felt the sting of lost, strained, and near impossible relationships. We have also known the sweet intimacy of a deep connection with our children. Sometimes all within the same day! Yes, being a dad can be tough, and we know because we walk the dad walk just like you. Whether you bask in the glory of a great father-child relationship, or struggle to connect, we've come together as dads, friends and most importantly, sons of God our Father to walk with you into a new season of improving, renewing or restoring your current relationship.

Our goal is to connect with you in the only way men truly bond, and that is by sharing truth. Sometimes that truth hurts, but that is also where healing, restoration and growth are found. While sharing this truth, we want to let you know that you are not alone in this journey called fatherhood. We all have the shoulders of the millions of dads who've come before us to stand upon, as well as accepting the mantle that each of us also influences this and future generations of fathers. This book will make sure you have the truths to become as solid of a father foundation as supernaturally possible.

Part of our past legacy is understanding that ever since the beginning of creation, the father effect has been in play. We'll talk about the Adam Life in another chapter, but when we consider the complexity of connection between father and child, we're taking it back to the original root. Seriously, who had a better relationship than Adam and God the Father? But guess what? They also had a falling out and it set a path for every relationship for generations up until yours.

The great thing about even broken relationships is that there's always the potential for reconciliation. It's also through Christ that you have a fast track to God the Father for repairing, rebuilding or continuing to grow your own relationships. We want to share with you what the Bible says about fatherhood, and because we are all men and brothers, we'll offer this in the spirit of 1 Corinthians 16:13-14:

> *"Be watchful, stand firm in the faith, act like men, be strong. Let all that you do be done in love."*

We know men like to think of themselves as completely independent creatures, capable of existing on their own. Well, that may be true in some cases, but if you're a dad, then complete independence is not the case. The truth is men seek bonding opportunities with other men. We draw strength from each other, and this is why we connect in sports, work, military, fitness, fraternities, social and civic organizations and just about anything that involves a club, team or league. Throw in a patch, jersey or logo and we're busting through walls like someone yelled out, "Hey, Kool-Aid!"

It's in this spirit of brotherhood that the four of us joined forces to share our lives, hearts and experiences (good and bad) with you—our brothers in the fraternity of fatherhood. We are as diverse in age, race, geography, occupations, relationships with our dads and with our kids as you can imagine. We know you'll be hard pressed to not identify with at least one of us, but probably all.

So that brings up the next topic. *Who are we?*

That's a great question. We're dads. You're probably saying, "Okay, Captain Obvious, but who has the pen and paper?" Fair enough. You'll get to know us as we move along because of the way we've structured this work.

Here's a quick thumbnail sketch of your authors—Richard Bright is a comedian, George Gregory is the chaplain for the Los Angeles Chargers, Juan Martinez is the senior pastor at Get Wrapped Church, and Scott Silverii is a retired Chief of Police.

Sure, there's more to us than this brief description, and because this book is not about us, let's not bore you with resumes. Since there are four of us writing this to you, we eventually grew tired of arm wrestling and flipping quarters to determine who wrote what. Instead, we've constructed the book in a unique way to best share our message and our personal perspectives.

Each chapter's topic will be addressed in two parts. Together, we write the first part covering the main subject. The next part is broken into four sections. We each write our own section that's told to you in our respective point of view. This allows us to share a unique perspective from our life and relationship with our own dads, and the bond and challenges with our kids.

It might sound like muddled instructions on the day of a surprise algebra exam, but trust us, it works. We've chosen the chapter topics because they've impacted our lives and we know for sure they have or will affect your life also. We don't proclaim to have all of the answers, but between four sets of eyes aimed at the same target, we're sure to hit the bullseye by sticking to God's Word and our honest experiences.

Ready? Aim. Fire!

*3 Children are a heritage from the Lord, offspring a reward from him.*
*4 Like arrows in the hands of a warrior are children born in one's youth.*
*5 Blessed is the man whose quiver is full of them. They will not be put to shame when they contend with their opponents in court.*
Psalm 127:3-5 (New International Version)

# FATHERS WHO MIRROR GOD

Did you know our first impression of God comes from our parents? Yes, even if you'd never heard of Him, by his loving nature, God created us for relationship with Him and in that model, He mirrors the way a loving parental connection is supposed to be. God is the perfect example for what it looks like to be a dad.

Now a few things to consider. The part of this book's title that reads, *One Perfect Father* isn't any of us who wrote this book, but God. Our desire should be to set our sights on *His* ways so that they become *our* ways in moving us toward being more perfect as a father. That's called modeling and it's how we learn to do either right or wrong. It's also why making a wise choice about who sets the example is so important. God the Father is that perfect example and by working to be like Him, we cannot go wrong.

We talk to men all of the time who feel as though they failed at fatherhood. They are quick to exclaim there's no training to be a dad, so you do the best you can. In reality, we only know what we know. If we grew up without a dad or had a bad example of what a godly dad should be, then all we know is that example. The beauty of grace is we're not trapped in that absence of a good example. There is a better way, and along with that is an actual instruction manual on fatherhood —the Bible.

The Bible is more than just an instruction manual. It's a love letter from the Father to His children. Have you ever written your child a love letter or told them precisely how you feel about them? See, that's something you can mirror right now, and we know your child will adore hearing your words as much as we should desire the words from our Father.

In God's love letter or instruction manual, we'll highlight ten characteristics of our Father that you can begin to mirror immediately. You may pick up on some that you are already doing an incredible job at—so great going Dad. Others might take an effort to get started, but please understand the power of each as they craft an amazing portrait of a godly dad. This isn't a chance but a choice. Maybe you've been a good dad and want to be great, or you've possibly dropped the ball but not the desire. The choice is yours and you have the God ordained power and heavenly authority to become a better dad.

Let's take a look at each and how they can apply to your life as a dad.

**Perfect Patience**

Have you ever snapped at your child for asking the exact same question one thousand times without even stopping to take a breath of air? Yeah, we know the feeling. Can you imagine how God the Father feels when we sin again and again and again? He even gave us His only beloved Son (John 3:16) so that we might come to know Him better. But still, we turn our backs or avoid Him altogether and yet God's love for us endures. Talk about enduring patience and compassion!

> *Praise the Lord. Give thanks to the Lord, for he is good; his love endures forever.*
> Psalm 106:1 (NIV)

Remain mindful if you know you're approaching a short fuse. It's okay to admit this because it's better than pretending you're an unending fountain of proverbial peace and patience. We all have our limits and children are masters at exploiting them faster than a late-night telemarketer. Pray for patience when you begin to feel angry or anxious. If you have to walk away to cool off, make sure your wife knows what you are feeling so that she doesn't think you're abandoning her or the situation with the kids. Also, be ready to extend her that same level of grace when she's about to bubble over.

We began by talking about the way God mirrors the example of a perfect Father. Example setting doesn't mean only showing the rehearsed or polished final product. It includes revealing the entire truth for the purpose of understanding that there is a process toward obtaining the goal. God's nature is love, but that doesn't mean He hasn't experienced other emotions (Genesis 6:6) bound within that nature. But the power of His example is that even when you've been pressed against the mat, or you still love but don't like your child's behavior at the moment, patience and kindness override anger and frustration. The key to this characteristic is that love always abounds.

Remember, anger is not a sin unless you sin in anger.

*22 The faithful love of the Lord never ends! His mercies never cease. 23 Great is his faithfulness; his mercies begin afresh each morning. 24 I say to myself, "The Lord is my inheritance; therefore, I will hope in him!"*
Lamentations 3:22-24 (New Living Translation)

**Perfect Timing**

When you feel totally overwhelmed and behind the eight-ball as time runs out, has it ever been helpful for others to remind you that we all have the same twenty-four hours in a day and that they get their stuff done plus some? We'd venture to say that it possibly makes you want to tell them where to stick their twenty-four hours. Yet the truth is, time is a precious resource and while you may not feel its powerful presence within your grip, it is indeed yours to invest as you choose.

One of the challenges of being a dad is being present in the lives of our kids. Showing up to an occasional ball game isn't the same as spending time playing catch or connecting during their favorite game. The challenge arises from balancing the demands of work, marriage, family and activities we enjoy participating in outside of being dad. Sometimes others use the competing interests against you to manipulate or attempt to shame you for deciding one activity over another. This verse from Ephesians should be your guide in determining which activities are a priority versus unwise pursuits that exhaust your most valuable resource.

*Pay careful attention, then, to how you walk—not as unwise people but as wise making the most of the time, because the days are evil. So don't be foolish but understand what the Lord's will is.*
Ephesians 5:15-17 (Christian Standard Bible)

God the Father created time but that doesn't mean He lavishes us in an unlimited amount of it. He is a God of order and structure. He separated the days from the nights while establishing time as a construct during creation. Within the boundaries of time, God makes the most use out of the time He created. You can choose to be just as efficient with your time and competing or conflicting interests.

Bible-based time management doesn't just happen anymore than thinking that waking your child up at midnight to play catch is a good idea. You must be intentional about time. There are unlimited ways to waste it, but so few chances to truly and purposefully channel it toward being dad. Begin to plan out your days and if you must go old school, break out the pencil (with eraser) and paper. Sketch out your day and then eliminate anything that detracts from those items you've deliberately labeled as priorities. Our guess is that social media and the internet are draining a huge chunk of time that could be reallocated to the kids.

Go RAD when evaluating your time. Reduce, Allocate or Delete (RAD) time spent on actions that produce a negative ROI (return on investment) such as social media surfing, late night TV scrolling and everything that sucks the life and time away from you and your child. It's your choice—choose wisely.

**Perfect Thoughtfulness**

If you had a dad who unselfishly gave his time and willingly sacrificed for you, then you have been blessed. In what is more akin to society's self-centered nature for personal gratification, a dad who exhibits Spirit-minded consideration for his child is a man after God's own heart. God the Father wants only and always what is best for you.

Why? Because you are His beloved child and just like any loving father, He wants to bless you.

*Since he did not spare even his own Son for us but gave him up for us all,*
*won't he also surely give us everything else?*
Romans 8:32 (Living Bible)

On the other hand, growing up with a dad who was consumed with his own pleasures may have taught you to look out for old number one before all others. Generational cycles are passed down because of the examples set by previous generations. God is the way maker and chain breaker. He wants to elevate you out of the pit comprised of poor examples and worse behavior.

God's perfect consideration for His child is designed to not only grace you with the gift of becoming closer to His perfect example of a Godly dad but guiding you toward healing from past pains caused by a non-attentive father. Additionally, He helps you spare your own child from growing up under the dark shadow of a dad who cared more about his game score than the desires of his child's heart.

Through God's example, you can start today by giving serious and intentional consideration to your child. It doesn't mean giving them everything they ask for, but the time spent listening and engaging them in real conversation will always be more appreciated and longer lasting than any gift you can afford.

**Perfect Approach**

Upping our dad game would benefit tremendously by making sure we are always approachable. We hear men say, "They can talk to me anytime." But the real question is, can they? Although you may be willing to set the remote down for a bit, do they know without a doubt that they can indeed approach you no matter what it is you are doing?

Father God gives a solid yes and amen to both of those. When you're in a relationship with His son, Jesus Christ, you have God's ear as well as His heart. He's never too busy for you, and before you say, "Yeah, but He's omniscient and should know what I want," understand that God made the decision to always be approachable because of His love for you. You, in the same manner, have the power to also make the choice to be truly approachable for your child. Just make sure they know it and whenever they decide to act upon it, you show it.

*He will not allow your foot to slip; He who keeps you will not slumber.*
Psalm 121:3 (New American Standard Bible)

**Perfect Choices**

A caring, mentoring dad is willing to allow their child to make their own choices. Now this doesn't mean encouraging a five-year-old to decide on a purchase of the family vehicle, but it does allow space for making decisions. Yes, there is growth even when the decisions are wrong, but not harmful. God our Father blessed us with the incredible gift of free will. While it's often the source of our own demise, had we not been given the opportunities to choose for ourselves, then how loving could that relationship actually be. As a matter of fact, God loves us so much that we are free to not choose Him.

*The heart of man plans his way, but the Lord establishes his steps.*
Proverbs 16:9 (ESV)

You can reflect God's love by encouraging your child to think critically about the choices they make. This also gives you both an opportunity to talk more often about things other than supper and the weather. One of the most common and harmful effects dads impart on their children is dominance. Dominant parents, usually the dad, create deficiencies in their children's behavior as they begin to engage in their own relationships.

You can begin showing this Godly trait immediately by talking to your child about the trust you have in their ability to think through the decision-making process. In that process, you should reinforce your willingness to remain approachable to discuss options and a final decision. This establishes you as the "resident expert" in all matters and allows you insight into their thinking as well as a chance to help influence their thoughts in a positive and affirming Christian direction.

*Train up a child in the way he should go: and when he is old, he will not depart from it.*
Proverbs 22:6 (KJV)

## Perfect Discipline

The word discipline is no one's favorite word. Unfortunately, it's often used out of context and within the negative connotation with punishment instead of instruction. Guess what? God applies both. The balance between teaching your child as a student of life and punishing them for breaking the rules is a constant search for the right rhythm.

Discipline's origin in the Latin root word is *disciplina* meaning, "instruction and training." It's a derivative from the root word *discere* —to learn. A disciple is therefore grounded in the Latin, *discipulus* meaning student.

*My son, despise not the chastening of the Lord; neither be weary of his correction: For whom the Lord loveth he correcteth; even as a father the son in whom he delighteth.*
Proverbs 3:11-12 (KJV)

To discipline means to teach, which is what God's Word does for us through the Bible. God teaches us by showing and explaining how to engage in a loving relationship with Him. But punishment is also an option when appropriate behavior is not exhibited. Just as God punishes us to correct our behavior, a loving dad must be willing to punish his child to ensure they return to a right posture and an appreciation for the rules as they understand the biblical principles of decisions and consequences.

*Whoever spares the rod hates their children, but the one who loves their children is careful to discipline them.*
Proverbs 13:24 (NIV)

Setting this into motion as a parenting skill requires constant self-assessment for making sure you're providing clear and adequate information at a level your child understands, allowing them the chance to ask questions for clarity and the care shown by detailing the expected outcomes and potential punishment for willfully bad behavior. This really is where leaning into God's Word and disciple-making examples are vital for ensuring you maintain a steady avenue for raising up young learners into adult leaders.

## Perfect Love

Even if all else fails in your efforts as dad, the one and most important lesson you can learn by mirroring God the Father is how to love. Unconditional and sacrificial are but two words to describe God's love. Even while God waited for us to recognize Him and enter into an intimate relationship, we continued to reject Him through sin. His love gave us the greatest gift in all the history of the world—Jesus Christ. That was also God the Father's deepest sacrifice.

Many dads grew up in a household where performance-based love was the daily diet of affirming affection. Be good, make good grades, listen to Mommy and Daddy, and all of the other hoops we were presented to jump through to earn praise and affection. God doesn't wait for us to impress Him. He comes running to us with arms wide open like the prodigal son's father. That's unwavering love.

---

## Richard's Session:

Quivering beneath my bed in horror as Dad screamed at Mom are the earliest memories I have of him. The sound of my mom crying still rings in my head and breaks my heart. I'd cover my ears as she begged my Dad to stop. Guilt doubled me over because I knew she was trying to protect me from his wrath over something I'd done or forgotten to do. This nightly scenario almost always ended with my mom trying to talk me out from beneath the bed. Even her loving promises lost appeal thanks to my fear of being harmed by my Dad and the ugly truth of being covered in urine.

Too frightened to chance sneaking to the bathroom, I'd cower in bed until my bladder failed. His loud, harsh threats slammed throughout our home and nailed me to my bed in fear. It was a weekly occurrence. In my Dad's wisdom, he decided to hang the pee-stained sheets on the front door for the world to see. I know it was mostly my family and friends, but that was my world as a child and the shame of it only reinforced the fact that I felt like a worthless loser.

"What's wrong with you?" he'd taunt. "Real men don't pee in the bed." That really drove home the message that I wasn't a real man. What I could not know at that time was that my Dad was bipolar and a raging alcoholic. What I did know at that time was to a little boy who spent more time in fear than playing outside, I was a huge disappointment to him.

As I got older, it was fairly obvious that the men in my family drank alcohol. Maybe it was the 1970's and real men measured their machismo by how much and how often they guzzled booze. Since all you know is all you know, I learned that a mark of being a real man was to drink. To make up for being the disappointment to my Dad, I thought that learning to drink alcohol would make him proud of me, a real man.

I remember my Dad's stories of him growing up during the depression and that even in the worst of times he turned out to be a great athlete. Football was his sport, and he went on to play for Stanford before trying out for the Chicago Bears. Although too small to make it in the NFL, he took great pride in his physical prowess. Even the many fights he bragged about always had him as the victor.

Of course, I took that as a clue to become an athlete if I wanted his attention. I wouldn't say I was headed to the NFL, but the Wynn Seale Buckaroos were a pretty good team. It was sure to draw his love and admiration as I caught, ran, blocked and tackled with reckless abandon. Do you know who Moya was? He was the kid who my Dad would cheer on when he decided to actually show up to my games. Anything I did on the field was criticized and compared to Moya. Did I hate Moya? No, he was my friend, but I learned that no matter what I tried to do, it would never be good enough to earn my Dad's love.

Earned love is not mirroring the way God loves us, but I had no clue who God was at that time and all I knew was that I'd do anything to get my Dad's approval. He did tell me on occasion that he loved me, but I never bought it. His words never set right with my spirit. There was no compassion, empathy or general concern about me.

Even today when I think back to being a kid, I can still hear him saying, "You wanna cry? I'll give you something to cry about." How come those words are what I remember? I'm so thankful that now when I listen to God the Father, all I hear Him say is, "I love you dearly, my son."

## George's Session:

One of my professors at Duke Divinity School taught me a lesson that I will never forget. While in class one day he said an interesting phrase. "We are all crooked sticks trying to make straight lines." As a student of theology and glutton for academic punishment, he reinforced a profoundly valuable lesson that day. We are not perfect. In our feeble attempts of living "good" lives, we are perfectly imperfect, crooked and flawed in our nature. Yet in our imperfect ways we strive to be like our perfect heavenly Father.

As a son, husband and father of two kids, I know I am far from being perfect. As my grandfather used to say, "my issues have issues." I sometimes lose my patience, get upset, and from time to time throw manly temper tantrums. Yes, I am far from perfect and yet I aspired to be perfect. Well, maybe not perfect but I certainly work hard at trying to be better. I believe deep down inside every man knows he's not perfect. Yet within each one of us is a God given desire to improve and get better than we were the day before. It's etched in our DNA.

I couldn't agree more that parents give us our first impression of God. My parents, Henry and Coleen Gregory, were great models and examples of what God must be like from an earthly perspective. They were married 52 years before my Dad went home to be with the Lord in 2020. Through their more than a half century being married, my siblings and I learned a great deal of what it's like to ask and seek forgiveness, honor the sacred covenant of marriage and stay together no matter what. I can honestly say that our national marriage ministry platform, Journey for Life, is based on their marriage and example for how God wants couples to love, honor and respect each other.

Like many kids growing up my Dad was my hero. Don't get me wrong there were times when we got into it, or he disciplined us above what I felt was needed. He had his issues with workaholic syndrome and could have honestly been there more for our extracurricular activities. And yet he was my hero. I'll let you in on a little secret—he still is. His good nature far outweighed his bad. To know him was to love him. I think in large part most people adored him because he walked to a drumbeat that was not his own. From early childhood my Dad committed his life to Jesus and tried to live his entire life knowing one important thing: his life was not his own and his daily actions should line up with his heavenly father's. He was truly a man and father who mirrored God.

Like my Dad, the reality hits me every day when I wake up that my life is not my own. I am called to live as a son of the Most High. While I am not perfect, my desire every day is to be better than the day before. Be a better husband, father, neighbor and leader. Be more patient, thoughtful, approachable, caring and lover of all but mostly to the few that matter that most: my wife and kids. I'll have to admit I have a long way to go. But I'm up for the challenge and my hope is you are too!

I saw a sign recently on a building that was being renovated that read, "Under construction. Work in progress." Let me remind you today, we are all under construction. We are all a work in progress.

### Juan's Session:

Sitting here thinking of how to even begin talking about my father has me shifting around in my chair as deep and once suppressed feelings begin to rise up from the depth of my soul. I allowed the tears to trickle across my face because it's the only relief I know I'll get. Honestly, I want to honor my Dad in this book because that's what fatherhood is supposed to look like, right? Instead, the tides of rage and despair keep forcing their way to the surface. Finally, I whispered in the quiet, "Why weren't you there for me?"

I shoved the laptop away and grabbed my cell phone. Waiting until my chest stopped heaving in the wave of grief that again gripped me, I wanted to dial his number. I'm an adult and I have every ability to call my Dad, but I tossed the phone back onto the bed. How could I expect him to answer that question? He never came to one of my ball games, and yet the reason I played was in hopes of earning his attention, his approval, his love.

There'd be no writing that day. All I could do was slump over onto my desk and lay my face over crossed arms as both shoulders rolled with each gasp for air. Time does not heal all wounds, and as I still grieve the loss of a relationship with my Dad, I now understand that it wasn't batting instruction or game attendance I wanted. I needed my father's love.

I will be obedient to God's Word and honor my father, but that honor will come through sharing the truth and still loving him enough to forgive him. It was impossible for eight-year-old me to reconcile that my Dad preferred women, money and the party life instead of me and my mom back at home. I misunderstood what role a father was ordained to play in his family's life because I confused our Puerto Rican culture of dancing, music and partying with a healthy home life.

That confusion abruptly ended the façade of our happy home when my father was caught in adultery with the woman upstairs. I'll never forget my mom and me walking out, and at eight years old thinking I had not only lost my Dad, but now I was the man of the household. Yes, confusing was the right word. The years that followed didn't help bring light to the darkness I was living in. Even custody and visitation orders meant nothing to him as he avoided ball games and school activities.

Even as I sit here in the room four decades later, finding comfort hearing my wife, Ruthy, out in the kitchen, there's nothing I wouldn't have given back then to hear my Dad say, "Well done," or "I'm proud of you, son." No, instead of words of affirmation, I would connect with my Dad over drinking alcohol and partying. It was so destructive, but when you're desperate for love, you'll do anything for it.

Performance based relationships are toxic. God didn't design the connection between father and son to be based on good behavior. God loves us no matter what we do or don't do. The problem with lost people is that we don't know God and therefore we can't possibly expect to live life as He intended it to be. Sure, we have a deep desire for love and an aching wound from rejection, but without God we simply see ourselves as broken and unworthy of being loved.

In my season of desperation for a relationship with my Dad, he'd really seemed to be willing to come through for me. I was so happy that finally I'd have my Dad back. Drugs had consumed my life and it was all I could do to hang on from one high to the next. My Dad said that if I got sober and clean, I could come live with him and that he had a job lined up for me. Finally, we were going to be that happy father and son.

I dove into a recovery program because I wanted to make him proud of his son. With about two weeks left in the program, I was rock solid and ready to walk out of there with a new, clear vision and a purpose for life. I still recall listening to the phone ring as I anticipated his voice on the other end. I was ready to come home to my Daddy.

As best I can still remember that call went like this:

"Dad, I'm almost done."

"Yeah."

"I can't wait to move in with you and get to work."

"Move in with me? I got a new girlfriend living here. You can't come here."

To say that I was crushed to dust would be an understatement. Recovery was the last thing on my mind, and I ran out because the only reason I agreed to it in the first place was to please my Dad. Instead, I hated him and seethed in anger at the man who had once again proven he couldn't keep his word or show his love. This wasn't a little league baseball game that he'd bailed out on because of some unknown woman. It was my very life, and his rejection created a monster in me that sought to destroy him by destroying myself.

Dad, I want to share with you that this isn't the way God designed it. He is a good Father who is always there with us. He loves us and adores us. If you had a broken relationship with your own dad or you currently are in a toxic relationship with your own kid, please understand that God wants to restore those connections.

Even in the crushed dust that was my life, my Dad once again rejected me. But it was God who reformed me, leaned into me and breathed new life into me. When I finally did come back into a renewed life through Christ, guess what I saw? No, not the years of addiction, depression and defeat. I was looking face-to-face with my Father who had just given me the gift of a new life. God will give you that same gift if you are willing to receive it.

Let me wrap up by saying that my intention was to be honest and still honor my Dad. The reason I've prayed over this message, and shared my story although it's tough to tell, is that if you never heal from what hurt you, you'll end up bleeding on people who didn't cut you. That usually means your kids will pay the price of your pain. We must forgive our fathers so that we can become good fathers.

### Scott's Session:

The relationship with my Dad looked nothing like the way God loves me. Although I had no idea who God was throughout childhood, I still sensed His presence in my heart. Even in the darkest of dark, God finds a way to pierce that void with His light. Growing up godless, my parents never once took us to church, prayed or mentioned the name God unless there was a curse word following it. I'd heard of God but once talk turned toward him being a Father, Son and Holy Spirit I wanted nothing to do with what I thought was spooky.

It's confusing and complicated for kids because God's design for family includes the earthly dad serving as the role of introducing his kids to what a loving father is supposed to be. When executed as God designed it, dads would mirror God the Father's nature and in that expression of headship, mentoring and love; the children would come to know God the loving Father.

In the same way Jesus reflected the light off of Him and toward his Father, earthly dads are responsible for directing the attention, adoration and desire for a deeply intimate relationship toward God the Father. It doesn't diminish the shine in a kid's eye for their dad. As a matter of fact, it enhances it.

When that design is corrupted by parents who raise their family outside of God's presence, then the only information we have about God the Father is what we see modeled by our parents. Because my first impression of God was a result of how my Dad treated me, I wanted nothing to do with either.

I grew up in a dysfunctional home of abuse, addiction and violence where there was no fatherly modeling of God's loving nature. I grew to see God the Father in the same distant, detached, and violent light as my Dad. I lived in fear as my Dad lurked in anticipation of catching me messing up as an excuse to punish and hurt me. His presence was dominating, so why wouldn't God be the same way? Wasn't He sitting so far away waiting to strike us down for messing up? Therefore, in my messed-up thinking, avoiding both God and my Dad was the best way to prevent agony.

One of the most painful parts of growing up with a dad that failed to mirror God, was never knowing the love or affirmation we all so deeply desire. My Dad never said he loved me, or really anything remotely nice to me. The words that quickly come to mind when I think of my childhood are, "You want a backhand?" I mean seriously, how's a child supposed to answer that?

I never realized the damage he'd rooted in my life by withholding those three little words—I love you. It sent me off the rails seeking affirmation in all of the wrong places. It wasn't until a few years ago as my Dad lay dying in a hospital bed that I gave one last effort to pull those words from him. I needed to hear them, or at the very least just to hear him say something decent to me.

Over the course of three days, I set up camp at his hospital bedside and prayed for those words of affirmation from my Dad. I didn't care about the years of neglect or abuse; I needed those words. In brief moments of clarity as he slipped into and out of consciousness, I even tried manipulating him to say I love you, but nothing. On the third day as the medical staff prepared us for his very soon passing, I remained pressed in as I understood the urgency of time and opportunity slipping away. With my Dad's last breaths, he took those very dear and dearly needed words to the grave with him.

It hurt then and it still hurts now, but what it did was help point me in the one direction my Dad had never done before—to God the Father. I'd given my life to Christ decades before my Dad's death, but the stronghold of hurting over the absence of his loving affirmation was finally shattered. I don't blame my Dad and I've forgiven him for the destructive life patterns that first began in my chaotic childhood.

Forgiveness has also freed me to focus my attention on the Father who doesn't have to *mirror* the Father because He *is* the Father. If you are struggling with a father wound from the past, now is the perfect opportunity to reset your eyes upon God the Father. He is perfect and loves us as the Father should.

# 2

# FATHERS WHO AREN'T TV DADS

Who's up for a challenge? Who are we kidding? We're men and always up for the challenge of competition. Name one dad character from mainstream television, movies or mass media that's portrayed as a Godly father. Our guess is that you'll go through a long list of programs where the dad character is portrayed as more of a prop or butt of the joke than the spiritual head of his family.

Modeling is an important part of the way by which we learn. How'd you learn to throw a ball, or cast a line, or grab the last slice of pizza? You saw someone else do it and you gave it a shot. Maybe it worked or not, but the seed of doing was planted. The next step was to keep imitating what you saw until you became proficient at it, or someone (hopefully your dad), stepped up to teach you the right way.

God's design for teaching us how to be a perfect dad is through modeling. We read about God the Father to get to know Him. We watch the way He interacts with His children (us) so we see how He handles the same situations we all encounter as dads. Next, we mirror His ways until they become our ways while the Holy Spirit helps coach you along the way to becoming a Godly dad.

The problem with media's mass appeal of the hapless dad characterization is that it stands in direct defiance to God's illustration of Father. He leads the way by moving in our lives as the perfect Father. He wrote an incredibly powerful instruction manual (the Bible) on fatherhood and even left a "life coach" in the Holy Spirit to help us see His example and understand His words.

Seems like our job of being dad should be pretty simple right? If it was, there'd be no reason for this book. Unfortunately, instead of relying solely on God for wise instruction, we've focused our attention on what the world says about how to be dad. We all watched TV dads and now our children consume a steady diet of media where kids rule at the manipulation of the mom character and the domination over an aloof portrayal of dad. It's destructive to the family and harmful to society to perceive every dad painted as incompetent, uninvolved or absent. But the truth is, popular programming's writers draw on current inspiration as much as creative expression.

Is this a case of life imitating art or the other way around? It's a difference of Ozzie and Harriet versus Ozzy Osbourne—a contradiction that can only be explained as cultural illustrations of how the family dynamics have changed. So, ask yourself again: Why are the majority of dads portrayed in film and commercials in need of rescue by mom or at the will of the kids?

Let's take a quick walk back through television history as it's compared to the culture of the respective decade. It's an interesting observation and also sheds light on why we seldom see dads cast as capable heads of their household.

**1950s:**

- Nuclear family dominates society with a 15% divorce rate and over 93% of homes with both parents present.

- *The Adventures of Ozzie & Harriet* which runs for twenty-eight years over radio and TV represents the ideal American family. Ozzie, the dad, is firmly the responsible and capable head of his household. Focus on family stability.

**1960s:**

- Nuclear family remains dominant but undercurrents of social rebellion inspired by race issues, Vietnam and what is termed the Generation Gap begin to surface. Two parent homes still rank at 90.9%.

- Most popular media portrayals include *The Munsters* and *The Flintstones*. Despite the obvious fact that neither father figure was human, both dad characters were bumbling, childlike lackies dominated by strong wives.

- This decade also saw the introduction of single-father sitcoms despite the national demographic of father-as-the-only-parent homes was below 3%. Shows such as, *Bonanza*, *The Courtship of Eddie's Father* and *My Three Sons* were popular and presented the dad as competent, nurturing and capable, but single.

**1970s:**

- Cultural holdovers from the 60's ideas such as sexual freedom, recreational drug use and countercultural music, hair and fashion styles emerge. Divorce rate rises to 25% as inflation forces mothers out of the home and into the workplace. The traditional nuclear family is under attack as 88.6% of homes have both parents present.

- Entertainment imitates the emerging trends as *The Brady Bunch* dominates the airways. A variant to the suburban ideal first introduced by *The Adventures of Ozzie & Harriet*, Mike and Carol Brady were cast to portray the real-world increase of blended families as a result of more divorce.

- A reflection of the times also introduced Archie Bunker's *All in the Family* that dealt with cultural challenges of the day. Although the '70s marked two-parent working households, *All in the Family* featured one unemployed parent, and life in a mixed-race community. Continuing to mirror the vastly different decade, *One Day at a Time* featured a working, divorced mother raising two children on her own. During this decade, more than 5.5 million households were managed by single mothers.

**1980s:**

- A more conservative era both politically and culturally, the 80's experienced a surge of single parent homes. Two-parent homes dropped to 80%.

- Media reflected the decade of conservative representations as families again centered around the parents. Shows like *The Cosby Show, Rosanne* and *Family Ties* explode as some of the most watched sitcoms of all time. All three shows presented dads as loving, leading and capable men, although the mother characters were also portrayed as very strong women who more often than not had to help, nudge or rescue their husbands from sticky situations.

**1990s:**

- Although marriages are ending in divorce 50% of the time, the economy is booming. Two-parent homes continue to decline at 75%. Disposable income increases personal mobility and causes families to spend more time apart than ever.

- Television's super family is *The Simpsons*. The dad figure, Homer is possibly the worst illustration of a father figure as the mother Marge raises three kids and him.

**2000s:**

- Divorce rates remain at around 50%, but two-parent homes have dropped to 72% as adult children remain in their parents' home well into their thirties. Tough economic times contribute to the boomerang effect of kids completing college but unable to find jobs, so they return home.

- Television returns to Ozzy. Not Ozzie Nelson, but Ozzy Osbourne. Although a semi-reality sitcom featuring the real-life family, the Osbournes present television audiences with a surprisingly traditional look at family. Another nontraditional premise featuring a solid father figure was *The Bernie Mac Show*. A real-life comedian who raised his sister's children while she battled drug abuse. Despite the reality reflected about America's drug war, Mac made for a positive surrogate representation.

In an article highlighting advertising media and the portrayal of dads titled, *Americans' View of Fathers' Competency as Parents Through a Mass Media Lens* it was revealed that fathers are overwhelmingly shown to be "foolish, no matter what race or socioeconomic status is depicted." Marketing and product branding in commercials also showed "when fathers were included in commercials, none of them were portrayed as nurturers whereas half of mothers were portrayed as nurturers."

While it might make for funny Super Bowl commercials, the way dads are portrayed in media has an impact on the way real dads are perceived by their children. It's vital that the paternal bond kids naturally develop with their dads is not impeded by character misrepresentations of incompetence. Kids who grow up with dads actively engaged in their lives overwhelmingly develop healthier across all social, mental, emotional, economic and spiritual demographics.

The more engaged we dads are in the lives of our kids, the better positioned we are in to monitor their media programming choices to ensure that they are not ingesting a steady diet of incompetent father characterizations. Refuse to allow negative media modeling to undo the investment you've made into building a positive father-child relationship.

And we'd be doing you a disservice if we didn't loop this conversation back to where we began—reality. Too many dads are absent, incompetent and passive secondary figures in the lives of their children. While we should never allow mass media to distort the reality of our best efforts at being a strong father, we sure can't expect television to create something in our parenting that we aren't. We cannot continue to depend on television to raise our kids. Instead, we want to coach you how to rely on the ultimate guide to alpha fatherhood—God's Word.

### George's Session:

I think we can all agree that there are no perfect dads. We all have things to work and improve upon daily. In fact, a mentor once told me that we never graduate from trying to become a better dad. TV dads and media, although entertaining, have never been and will never be the best source for modeling fatherhood in its purest form. We need much more than a few moments from the click of a channel to understand the full extent of fatherhood. Instead, we need real, committed, and focused dads to teach and model what good dads are supposed to be on a daily basis. For that to happen we need a few key ingredients —presence, time and a sense of responsibility!

I might be dating myself, but I remember watching most of the TV dads listed above as I grew up watching TV and paying attention to media. What saddens me as an African American father is the somewhat negative view of African American dads that I've seen portrayed in media news and on TV screens across the decades. In watching the media, one could falsely assume that the large majority of African American dads are absentee, incarcerated or too inept to have stewardship of their family.

In 2008 former President Barack Obama gave a Father's Day sermon at a church in Chicago in which he said, "Any fool can have a child. That doesn't make you a father. It's the courage to raise a child that makes you a father." Obama went on to make a critical point when he said, "A father's responsibilities don't end at conception." These words are a powerful challenge to all fathers both new and old. We don't need TV dads or media framing what real fathers are supposed to be. We simply need present dads willing to own their responsibility and put in the time and effort of raising kids.

One of the things I'm most grateful for in life is having a present dad growing up. A dad who was there to help me when I needed direction and correction. A dad that would shower me with love and was there for me during times when I was afraid. I know for many this is not the case which is why I am sincerely thankful for his example. I'm thankful for a dad that invested time in learning how to be a good dad, not because he did everything right but because he wasn't too proud to admit when he was wrong. I am grateful for all the times that he drilled it into my head that real men handle their responsibility and do not make excuses.

For years I watched his example but there was a day when simply watching was not enough, I had to follow his example. In 1995 just before my last semester in college, my now wife but then girlfriend invited me over to let me know she was pregnant with my child. As you can imagine I was not ready at all to be a dad. I was months from graduating with school loan debt and no job lined up to support myself let alone a child or family. What should have been one of the happiest days of my life was actually one of the scariest. In that timid moment of reality, I never wondered what a TV dad would do if he were in my shoes. Nope. Instead, I thought about what my Dad actually did for me and my siblings. He showed up every day and displayed a strong symbol of presence, commitment and responsibility.

Well, if you know me you know the end of this story. With my knees knocking I married my then girlfriend and we've been happily married for twenty-five years. And the little life that we conceived is now a twenty-five-year-old man and we call him Jay. I often wonder what life would be like if I took my cues from culture or media. Many would say just abort or abandon the kid and wait until you are ready to be a father and a husband. No way!

Although financially and maturity-wise I was not "ready," I did have an example to draw from that no reality TV show can teach. I had the example of a loving and committed dad that has guided me along the way.

### Juan's Session:

I became a father at a very early age. I'd just gotten out of high school and she was still in her senior year. When I tell you that we were on our own, I'm not exaggerating. Part of being isolated also meant getting no advice on fatherhood other than I'd better get a job and get married. Back then I figured I was man enough to make a baby, so I was man enough to be a man.

I defaulted to do just like my Dad had done. Why? Because all we know is what we know. Without having the benefit of a better way, I clung to what I was taught as a child. The crazy thing was that after my Dad walked away from my mom and me, I turned to the television for my Dad fix. When we read in Proverbs 22:6 about training up a child in the way they should go, that equally means that if they are taught good, they will return to good and if they knew bad, that they would lean on bad. I did what I was trained to do.

Looking at the long game in parenting, unless kids are trained through godly instruction and discipline, their bad behavior will follow them right into adulthood. Discipline is not meant to crush the spirit of a child but to break their ill will so that they follow the right path. Instead of Bible teaching, I turned to TV, but the dads I watched were like cartoon people. They didn't look, talk or act like any man I knew so I disregarded them as jokes.

The movies were where I found my model for being a man. *Scarface* lit my spirit on fire and immediately I knew that was what a real man was and who I wanted to be. Rappers in my day banged on about manhood and how real men were supposed to act, and without anything real to show me otherwise, I believed them. In my world, the men I knew, yes, even my own Dad were just like the macho men in the rap songs, so it had to be true.

With that false understanding of what being a man and a dad looked like, I walked away. Not only did I abandon my first wife, but also my two sons as well. My walking away also cost my second son and me nineteen years of not knowing anything about each other. How do you explain to your child that what their dad learned about fatherhood was from movies and music? I'm not proud of that.

You'd have thought I'd learned my lesson after losing my marriage and family, but it wasn't long until I was exercising the very same crooked patterns that I'd first learned as a child. My daughter was born and although I wanted to do better, I didn't know how. Soon, I abandoned her too. I'm not proud of that either.

The beauty of having a relationship with God the Father is that He freed me from the wrong ideas about what a father was. All of the lies in the movies and music that had saturated my soul and guided my missteps were shattered as God began to teach me how to father. Once I learned from my Father what a true, pure version of being a father looked like, God restored my family. Today, thanks to God the perfect Father, I have a great relationship with my children.

The Bible says in Job 42:10 that once God restored him, He gave him twice as much as he had before. God blessed me with a double portion as well thanks to my wife Ruthy and her three kids. In that restoration God returned me to my ordained position as their father, and in that authority, I get to teach them about God's love. I simply mirror God's actions to the best of my ability. They get to witness what a changed heart looks like not just by words or television, but in real life.

I am grateful today for the fathers who are in Christ because together we can bring change in our homes, which will then transfer over to the Church and community. We get to reproduce the spirit of the living God.

### Scott's Session:

I really had no idea what I was doing. Prior to my first son's birth, I was naturally nervous, but somewhat naively optimistic that I'd figure it out. The advice I received from others usually included vague encouragement like "You'll just know when the time comes" or "leave it to the mother," plus a few other really knuckle-headed suggestions. The truth was no one I sought out actually had a grasp for how to do fatherhood.

The one decision I made before my son was born was to not do anything the way my Dad had done with me. Like most of us, I grew up watching television dominated by a vast range of father figures from Fred Flintstone to Dr. Huxtable of *The Cosby Show*. We learn by imitating what is modeled. Because my childhood had provided mostly examples of what not to do, I sought out examples for how to be a good dad.

We do what we see, and thanks to the disingenuous characterizations of television and movie dads, I was left with a void. So, what did I do? I did just what the others who had given such thin advice told me to do. I tried to figure it out on my own. The problem with that is wherever there is a void, it will be filled. My void was created by not having a positive Christian example of fathering, as well as a tendency for defaulting back to what I knew. Whether good or bad, we naturally return to where we've been.

I loved my son and showered him with hugs and words of affirmation, but gradually I slipped into the only patterns I'd known as shown by my Dad who'd focused on work, hobbies and anything else other than his kids. The crazy thing is, we try to attach a tangible reality to the fantasy of TV dads, but they are just that—fantasy. I could no more be

Mike Brady from watching his bunch than I could turn into a Corvette by sitting in my garage. So, what did I do? I unintentionally emulated my Dad by isolating myself from family through work and activities away from them.

It wouldn't come until years later that I was able to break away from that authoritarian, provider mode and freely share my heart with my kids as God the Father shared His heart with me. Having the example and the daily love of God the Father is a powerful opportunity for breaking free from past strongholds and negative systems set in your life.

If you are in need of a positive father role model, try turning off the television and social media. Get connected with men in your community who are mentors. Good, kind, decent Christian men who have led their family with Bible-based truths are always willing to raise up spiritual sons. But you must be willing to come under their authority of leadership and teaching. When I met my spiritual father, it filled a massive void and began to repair the wounds left unattended from my past. Just the loving affirmation can ignite the light of Christ in your life that will shine bright into the lives of your family. God did not design us to be Homer Simpson. We were created to be Dad!

### Richard's Session:

I remember being a kid back when *Leave It to Beaver* was a number one show to watch. I adored the brotherly love between Wally and the Beave because my brother and I were very close even though I was 5 years older than him.

In my eyes, Ward Cleaver was the best dad ever because he always showed patient understanding even when the boys messed up or got into trouble. Ward was what I wanted in my Dad, but unlike the fantasy of television, my Dad's explosive over-reactions often sent him into fits of rage and yelling. Each time he flipped into a reactive rage of emotion, instead of a measured fatherly response, he surrendered his authority as our Dad and became "that guy."

Because of his behavior, he usually acted worse than whatever it was my brother or I did to make him respond like that. Even as a young boy, I wanted a father who held my respect and trust through his paternal authority. I never found that in my home, so I stayed glued to the tube watching Ward Cleaver. Sure, I knew it was make-believe, but when fake is better than reality, you cling to the charade. Unfortunately, setting the bar for my own Dad by watching endless hours of a television family only made the daily disappointments hurt worse each time my Dad failed to deliver on even the most basic of genuine emotions.

I also associated God the Father with the only father in my life. I became as disappointed in Him as I was in my Dad. That might sound odd, but once you realize that our first understanding of God actually comes from the way we relate to our dad you can see where I'm coming from. All you know is what you know, and what I knew was that my Dad caused me pain. Why would I believe God would be any different as a father?

The inconsistency of my daily life left me unstable while trying to please my Dad while also trying to stay out of his crosshairs. Unlike the ideal Ward Cleaver, my Dad dominated us by controlling everything. So much for free will and exploration as kids. I mean seriously, I wasn't even allowed to order food or salad dressing without my Dad telling me what I would or wouldn't do.

It might seem trivial, but as a child those interactions of being stifled at every turn really caused me to withdraw and of course, rebel. Simple tasks became monumental confrontations. I recall being in a restaurant and asking for the steak to be cooked medium well. Not a big deal right? I guess it was to my Dad as he belted out, "No, he wants it well done." I was so embarrassed. Sure, I was thankful to have steak but at what cost? Even controlling the type of salad dressing I could use was yet another way of dominating me as a child. I know now that it was his way of controlling other people and was something he took great joy in doing—even his wife and kids.

I soon began to take on the persona of Eddie Haskell because fooling others into thinking I was the perfect kid was the only way I could hide the hurt of a dysfunctional home. Once again, inconsistency was ruining my life. It was literally the shifting sands mentioned in Matthew 7:24-27 because nothing was as it appeared. Even when I garnered the courage to ask my Dad about his decisions so that I might follow them to the letter of his law, I was confronted with spankings for questioning his authority or condemned with the "Do as I say not as I do" speech. Talk about confusing. So, I did what caused the least pain by avoiding my Dad and the God I couldn't understand for allowing my life to be so jacked up.

I'll tell what hurt me then and still does to this day is when I talk to other men about their experiences with their dads. I used to tell the men who grew up without a dad in their life that they were fortunate to have escaped the life I dealt with. Their typical response was that they would've preferred to have at least had a dad that treated them badly as opposed to not having one at all. That reality really hurt, and it drove me to make a bunch of internal vows about how I was going to behave once I became a father.

Internal vows never lead to positive outcomes because instead of leaning on God to make tangible change, we depend on our own ability. I'd have to say my style of fatherhood ended up being more like Al Bundy on Married with Children. Yeah, don't judge because I'm sure I'm not the only man out there who can say the same thing. Many of us dads excuse our behavior by blaming it on the bad examples or lack of any example while growing up. That doesn't make it right. It makes us lazy. Continuing bad behavior as a father because it's what we saw as a child is a lie, and it's what I used to believe.

I used to be that dad with a TV remote control in one hand and a beer in the other. I was plenty content allowing my wife to raise the kids. I did as little as possible. It's called passive male syndrome. Sure, my childhood sucked but that didn't make it right to curse my kids with the same legacy. We all have a better person inside us, but we can only bring it out by the grace of the Holy Spirit who lives within each of us.

Never once in seventeen years of marriage to my first wife did I ever pray with her or the kids. There was no deeper connection to my family beyond simply existing in the same house day to day. It was easy to be an Al Bundy, always looking at the ladies, wanting to drink beer and make fun of my wife. I had no interest in being accountable to anything or anyone. It's the way my Dad behaved, but it didn't make it right for me to be a poor imitation of him. Where my focus should've been was attempting to be like God the Father.

I can't imagine being that way now, but back then I was giving the best of what I had to offer. That meant I didn't have much to give because I wasn't living for Christ. All I possessed were the broken pieces of a man my Dad had shattered years ago. It wasn't until God put those pieces back together and formed a dad that loved his kids the way God loves us that I fulfilled my potential.

I hope by now you can see that you have so much more to give, and so much more life to live. Being dad is an incredible honor and a blessing to both you and your kids. God has to be present in all things. Yes, He has to be your TV dad, your real-life dad and your spiritual dad. God the Father is your answer to everything.

Men, if you're on a journey of brokenness and need healing, now is the time to put the remote down, put the beer down, put the pornography down and get on your knees and confess to Jesus that you have made a mess of your life and you want to change. Let's stop being the dads on TV who are the butt of all the jokes. Let's dust ourselves off and be present in the lives of our wives, our children, our family, our friends, our co-workers and all who we come in contact with. We have to be different because we're not Ward Cleaver or Al Bundy. The truth is, we are God's children, and He has ordained you to serve in a very important role—Dad.

# 3

# FATHERS WHO LEAD IN LOVE

Thanks to very different experiences with regard to the relationships between us and our own dads, the realization of love being a choice looked extremely different. While some of us were shown a dad's decision to sacrificially love his family, the others struggled through the damage of what choosing not to love caused.

Love is not an emotion. Yeah, that tripped us up the first time we heard it. There were heavy doses of healthy debate over it. Sure, it's an emotion because we've always gotten that warm feeling when we just knew it had to be love. The truth is love is not an emotion and we are thankful that it's not.

We know it goes against conventional wisdom and cultural propaganda, but love is a choice. Our feelings are emotion-based and within that swirl of undulating experiences, we may think love is wrapped up within, but to love someone is to first make a decision to love them. Think we're off point? That's fair but think about this.

Who's your favorite sports team? Yeah, you love them until another losing season or boneheaded play that costs y'all the game. Sure, you'll go back to watch them next season, but right now, you've switched off the TV and are headed out of the house. That's the same way we treat people in our lives and it's not based on a soul-deep decision to love. It is a performance-based relationship. You win and I watch. You lose and I'll catch up on the news.

Can we be brutally honest here? This is the way most of us grow up. Make good grades, do your homework, clean up your room, be quiet while you're in the waiting room, and the list goes on. We learn to earn our parents' approval by doing good deeds.

It's all based on performance. Ever wonder why so many relationships go bad? Most often it's because the child, no matter how hard they try, can't, or will never fully satisfy a parent's demand for excellent performance. The standard of this so-called excellence is a moving target. If it was something tangible like doing twenty pushups a day, then there'd be a marker for success. In performance-based relationships the standard is whatever the dominant parent deems satisfactory at the moment.

That leads to dissatisfaction and eventually rejection by the parent. Unfortunately, this usually leads to long-lasting abandonment (emotional and/or physical) for the child. Your authors learned the vast differences resulting from a dad making that decision to love or a dad who based attention purely on performance and worst of all having a dad show or express zero love. Regardless of our respective experiences, we all were influenced by the decisions our dads made about love.

Love is unconditional. Loving unconditionally is a journey and not a destination. It's tough to say that you'll choose to love someone, no matter what they do. Seriously think about that for a moment; anything they do? No matter how bad, horrible, or traumatic, you'll love them? It takes effort and an excellent example of how to make it happen. Where do we find such an example of unconditional love?

The answer is God the Father. Isn't it incredible we don't have to look very far to discover an example for fathers who lead in love? What's even easier is that our perfect example is laid out in the most distributed book in the history of the world—the Bible. As a matter of fact, the entire book is a love letter from our Father to us. This letter talks about everything from finances to health, but no matter the topic, it's all about love. Yes, leading in love.

A father's impact is undeniable in the development of a child. Even before the kid comes to know God, their dad's presence is designed to be the number one big guy. Kids need a loving dad to lead them, not a demanding job site supervisor. The critical role of dad doesn't have to be figured out on your own. Looking to God's example as illustrated throughout the Bible gives you a rock-solid foundation for not only being the man of the house, but also being the big-hearted man of the house. Our kids depend on this for their spiritual and moral formation.

We'd like to make mention of something important as we've all tripped over it a time or two. It's easy to say, "be like God," but in the daily grind, we often fall short of that lofty, heavenly ideal. While that might challenge some men to buck up and try harder, it sends some dads off along a dark path pitted with the same old feelings of failure and guilt they were forced to grow up with. Like we said earlier, this is a journey not a destination. We'll quickly admit that the dads we are today are nothing at all like the dads we used to be. Thank God for that! So, if the Bible isn't downloading data dumps about dad-hood, don't stress over it. It's what inspired us to write this book.

Let's cover a few basics that'll help put you on track for picking out those principles best aligned with God the Father's example of leading in love.

### Love God First and Most

We've talked about whether our own dads did or did not mirror God through their lives and into ours. For them to have done that would've required that they first loved God more than themselves, their wife, and yes, you. Now this command goes to you also and if you truly want to lead in love as God the Father leads us, then do as Matthew 22:37-38 says; *"Jesus said unto him, Thou shalt love the Lord thy God with all thy heart, and with all thy soul, and with all thy mind. This is the first and great commandment."*

Too often we set our emotional focus on the wife and kids. Sometimes we set our sights on work, hobbies and friends, but those are also misaligned priorities. Anything we place above God becomes an idol and a god (lower case g). Yes, you can worship your kid and your golf clubs. God is very clear that there shall be no god before Him. Isaiah

43:10 and Exodus 20:3, *"Thou shalt have no other gods before me,"* means that God leaves no room for competition. God has before and will always remove false gods from your life, or He'll just leave you alone to worship your idols.

Setting your sites and heart on God the Father does not mean you love your kid any less. Actually, it gives you the capacity to love them with a deeper and more intimate level than surface emotions and paternal obligations. Want to love like God, then love God.

**Love Momma**

We are stepping lightly here because we understand you may or may not be married to your kid's mom. Regardless of the relationship you have or had with your kid's mother, it's still important to show love and respect toward her. Kids are emotionally proprietary about their parents. Even in situations of abuse or abandonment, loyalties may become confusing, but do run deep.

There is a spiritual hierarchy established for thriving in relationships. It's found in Ephesians 5:21-33 and is a great guide to lead and encourage you as the head and a leader of your household. When you love God above all, then you are able to illustrate His love for others and that includes mom. If you are married to your kid's mother, then Ephesians is your blueprint along with the entirety of the Bible.

If you and their biological mother are not married, have no relationship or possibly she has passed away, it's still important for you to show the love of God as an example for you child. Taking the Christ road in choosing to show love toward the other parent even within a negative atmosphere, allows your child to see exactly how God can love us even when we're not in perfect alignment with Him.

**Love Truth**

We relish the role as protector and warrior dad. We go to great lengths to keep our kids safe, and that might even include shielding them from the truth. There's an old adage people use to excuse or soften the guilt we feel when failing our kids. "Kids are resilient," has been used ad nauseum in divorce and child custody cases. It's what we say because we know our actions have consequences yet hope that doesn't extend to our kids. The reality is kids hurt and hurt deeply. Isn't that a part of why you're here too?

Loving our kids enough to always deal in truth is challenging for knowing the maturity levels of appropriateness, but also vital in maintaining an honest connection.

*Faithful are the wounds of a friend; profuse are the kisses of an enemy.*
Proverbs 27:6

There are times when we get to say "Yes" and others that we must say "No." Look, we get it. No one wants to disappoint their child but failing to deal straight and with authority only leaves them with instability and uncertainty when interacting with you. They might be unhappy with a no, but it's better than allowing them to get hurt with a yes.

The balance is reached through loving discernment, and ultimately, let your yeses be yes and nos be no. Being unable to give them a solid yes or no and stick to it gives the illusion you are open to their strongest manipulative efforts. Too many answers of yes and we become a pushover. Too many no's and, well, you get it. The proper posture as a dad who leads in love is to reply with honesty, clarity and always in love.

**Love Wisdom**

When we talk with men about what is wisdom and who is wise, we get responses ranging from being a grandfather to fictional characters like Dumbledore or Gandalf. The one thing most of us do have in common is that we seldom, if ever, think of ourselves as wise. Maybe that is wise, but God's design is that we do not neglect ourselves of the precious gift of wisdom. When you have time (hint, make the time) please read all of Proverbs 4: A Father's Advice About Wisdom.

And speaking of the book of Proverbs, it's all about what else but wisdom. God provides instruction through the Bible and particularly the Old Testament's book of Proverbs to guide us dads in a life of values, moral behavior and the very meaning of life. Because all wisdom begins with fear of God (loving submission to His will) it's the foundation upon which we must live life as a man, husband and father. Anything else and we're back to slinging through the muddy hallows of failure and despair.

*The fear of the Lord is the beginning of wisdom:*
*and the knowledge of the holy is understanding.*
Proverbs 9:10 (KJV)

Once you go all in for living your life for God, you will understand that through the Holy Spirit's indwelling and guidance, your thoughts begin to become higher than those of mere sports scores and who did what to whom on social media. Wisdom is in the way we live out our daily lives. It's having the wisdom to first love God and then receive His gift of wisdom. It's nothing we can earn or learn. There's a difference between reciting ancient Greek philosophers and living out the Word of the Lord our God. Make the wise choice in pursuing God and you will soon lead your own kid with wisdom. Choose wisely.

---

**Juan's Session:**

Think about how important the role of a Father is when we talk about leading in love. The Bible calls God our heavenly father, but He is also love because His very nature is that of love. In that love, He is the one perfect Father who gave His son for His children.

We as Fathers represent that heavenly picture on earth. We could never love like God the father without the cross of Jesus Christ. It's because of this absolute love that we can come to the end of ourselves daily and to the beginning of God's love where we become a new man. In order to lead in love we must follow Jesus and allow Him to lead us in our everyday decisions with our children, extending grace and mercy through our imperfections.

Similar to God the Father, our role as dad is defined through love, discipline and parenting, which is another word for discipleship and mentoring. Look at what the Bible says about God's discipline in

Hebrews 12:9-11. *"It's the child he loves that he disciplines; the child he embraces, he also corrects."*

God is educating you and that's why you must never drop out of dad class. He loves you and is treating you as dear children that He wants to raise up as a Godly dad. Don't back away from His instruction even when you feel as though you've failed or are walking apart from Him. What you feel isn't punishment, it's *training*. That's the normal experience of children being disciplined.

Only irresponsible dads leave children to fend for themselves. Would you prefer an irresponsible God? We respect our own parents for training and not spoiling us, so why not embrace God's training so we can truly *live*? While we were children, our parents did what seemed best to them. But God is doing what *is* best for us by training us to live God's holy best.

Sure, while we're in the middle of it, discipline isn't much fun. It always feels like it's going against the grain. Later, of course, it pays off big-time because it's the well-trained dads who find themselves mature in their relationship with God. Today, I'm having to do a lot of the things that I didn't do because I wasn't in my children's lives. So now they are adults and it's a bit more difficult. Well, a lot more (LOL) but I sit with them as we talk and I get to lead and disciple them in love.

*"One father is more than a hundred schoolmasters"* — George Herbert

It's what God does with us and it's what we should do with our children. There is no greater investment of our time as men than to put on your "dad hat" and sit with them, listen to them, encourage them and affirm them. Let them know you are always there for them and mean it, and when you mess up (and you will mess up), go to the cross of Christ to show them how you are led by love. In that example, ask your child for forgiveness and be the example you want your child to reproduce.

There's a Spanish story of a father and son who had become estranged. The son ran away, and the father set off to find him. He searched for months to no avail. Finally, in a last desperate effort to find him, the father put an ad in a Madrid newspaper. The ad read:

*Dear Paco,*

*Meet me in front of this newspaper office at noon on Saturday. All is forgiven.*

*I love you.*

*Your Father*

On that Saturday, eight hundred Pacos showed up looking for forgiveness and love from their fathers. There are many people looking for the love of the Father. You have the golden opportunity to show them what that looks like today.

### Scott's Session:

Leading in love requires a decision. If we waited until we felt like loving, then that wait could be never-ending and leave those in our lives hurting and in need of what we didn't feel like giving. And, if I can be respectfully honest, that's a load of bull. Waiting to see how you feel isn't love at all. Love is a choice. One of my dear spiritual dads always says, "Choose your love and love your choice."

That's what I decided to do, but it also required an understanding of love's hierarchy. I'm blessed that my wife, Leah understood that heavenly chain-of-command so to speak. We committed to a covenant marriage which meant my first choice was to love God above my wife and kids. Guess what? She wasn't offended or jealous or resentful. She'd also made the choice to love God above me and the kids.

Making that first and most important decision made the second decision even easier. My wife always comes second to God and before our kids. I know lots of people say their kids are their life and that's a mistake. In cases of blended families, biological parents often place their own kids above the new spouse. Any wonder why these marriages fail almost 60 to 70% of the time? Your kids must come third because raising them is a temporary assignment, but marriage was designed to last forever.

Once I decided to make the right alignment, the kids came to understand that while they are loved, they do not come before God or their mom. Dad, don't fear that they'll feel rejected. This is God's design and by placing your child above God, they in effect become little idols or demi-gods. And while they might enjoy bossing around adults, it really doesn't make for healthy relationships.

Leading in love and in the proper spiritual alignment has allowed me to model to my family the way God wants them to be loved. We want the kids to love God above us because while I have and will disappoint them at times, our upward focus on God the Father provides the space for grace in our screwups and the foundation of a Father who doesn't mess up. I don't ever try to compare or compete with God. I only choose to become more like Him by reflecting His nature in my own life. Making that decision allows me to know God the Father in a very personal relationship. It allows my wife to see me in a loving way of caring and humility and it allows my kids to know me as their example of what a loving father actually looks like in a daily walk.

That would not be possible if I waited to see if I felt like leading in love. That would lead to an unstable swing of emotions that subjected my wife, kids and me to an unhealthy existence and dysfunctional home. Instead, by focusing your love first on God and then your wife and next the kids, you become the steady rock that God designed you to be. You are rock solid because you are Dad.

### Richard's Session:

Going back to those inner vows I was talking about earlier; they are super hard if not impossible to break without God's help. An example of an inner vow would be if you grew up without money, so you tell yourself when you grow up you'll never be without money. You have just taken control of how you see, respect, earn, save, and spend money along with other things too. Another common scenario is someone who was spanked as a child and vowing to never discipline their kids. Guess what? Yep, you end up with unruly kids and a resentful spouse because you refuse to discipline them.

The issue with making inner vows is, God has to have complete control over every area of your life. Whenever you have an inner vow, you are telling God that you are in control instead of Him. That vow immediately sets you out of alignment with God's will and increases the potential for a corrupted experience with whatever the focus of your inner vow is.

One of my many inner vows was that I swore I'd love my children way better than my Dad loved me. They'd never fear me or question whether I loved them. Easy right? The problem was, I didn't know how to love the way God wanted me to love. The result was a jacked-up experiment that left my kids in a chaotic environment and one in which they still suffer the wounds as adults. It's only because of the love of God the Father that I learned to love like Him, and in return show that love to my adult kids.

A dear friend of mine, fabulous pastor and author Joel Malm, likes to share a Chinese proverb: "The best time to plant a tree is thirty years ago. The next best time to plant a tree is today." It's never too late to start because there's no expiration date on being dad.

Without God's help, you can only give the love to the level in which you feel loved or have been loved. My mom once shared that when I was four years old, I sat on her lap squeezed her face with my little hands, and asked her if she loved me? I was 54 years old when she told me this story. Surprised, a raging wave of anger rose up from deep in my soul. I asked my mom why would a four-year-old have to ask such a question if he wasn't feeling unloved? I was so hurt that she didn't have the insight at that time to detect the hurt I felt, but then I began to think about the love I give to my wife and kids. Were there times when they'd have to squeeze my face and ask if I love them?

For as long as I could recall, I felt alone. I carried the emptiness of feeling unloved and unlovable from broken relationship to broken relationship. My first marriage only ripped the scabs of those hollow feelings off of my heart as I continued to suffer through seventeen years until we divorced. During those post-divorce years, I struggled to connect with my kids, but because I had no foundation other than the pain of my empty childhood, I continued to hurt them the way I'd been hurt.

Again I tried to buy my children's love because I had learned no other way. I spent as much time with them as I could, but all my bad behavior got in the way, always. Even the good times were overshadowed by past hurts when we lead by our own understanding. I thought spending time and money on them would compensate to show my love where I wasn't able to express it. I was wrong. Sure, I told them that I loved them and encouraged them in life, but my words were empty because I wasn't showing them love.

When it came to praying with my kids, I failed there too. I mostly avoided it because I really didn't know who I was praying to. The crazy thing was that the one prayer I said with them was that horribly scary prayer. You know the one: "If I die before I wake, I pray the Lord my soul to take." Dang, I hated that as a kid, and yet there I was reciting it as a dad. Honestly, it was the only one I knew. You see, we can only teach from where we are and what we know, and if we don't know the love of God, we can't teach it.

Dad, we all have a story, and as a follower and believer in Christ it's important to share our testimonies with each other. If God can use a broken vessel like me, He can use you too. I was so lost that I thought the best way to love my children was to divorce their mother. When you base your decisions on emotion, which is a flesh motive, you will choose wrong all of the time. You see, God loves us no matter what we do, where we are, and what we believe. He loves us unconditionally.

Love gives at the expense of self, while lust takes at the expense of others. This is but one of the many lessons I've learned from attending classes to become a better dad, husband and human. Yes, we all need to continue to grow, especially in the area of learning to love like the Father. Love is such a great word that sometimes we take it for granted or in the wrong context. I love sandwiches, I love the beach, I love sports cars, I love my wife and I love my children.

You see what I mean that the word love can be inserted anywhere without having the true meaning. We say it just to say it because we've been conditioned to. As a dad and husband, I want to think about the word love and why I say it to my family and friends. Being a pastor, we say "love you" to people we don't even know. When I was first attending church and someone would approach me saying, "I love you," I didn't understand why they would say that to someone they didn't know. As I matured in my faith, I came to understand that they do love me because God first loved them, and me and yes, especially you.

I've also learned over time that people will disappoint you. Included on this list is definitely your spouse, parents, children, family, friends, bosses, teachers and the list goes on. I have the honor of officiating weddings and I always include a reading of 1 Corinthians 13:4-5 that says, *"Love is patient, love is kind, it does not envy, it does not boast, it's not proud. It does not dishonor, it's not self-seeking, it is not easily angered, it keeps no record of wrongs."* If we could just for a moment remember this passage when we are about to use the word love, it would start to give a true meaning of the word and start to change our hearts.

We all have heart conditions that we were born with called iniquity, or better known as sin. I can tell you from my own experience that God the Father does and can change your hard heart. I ask God daily to show me how to love my wife and family because the need to be loved is the meaning of life, but the way we feel love is different and unique to each of us. Don't worry whether or not you are showing love in the proper way. Focus on the act of loving rather than how it looks. More often than not, we love others in the way we need to be loved, but unfortunately, that's not always the way they receive love.

Dad, whether you've made impossible inner vows about the way you were going to treat or love you kid, and now find them impossible to honor, it's a great time to turn it over to God and ask Him to break you from those vows and show you how to love your family the way He loves you. If you're like me and have made a lot of screw ups, please know that 1 Peter 4:8 assures us that love covers a multitude of sins. It's never too late to plant that tree.

### George's Session:

As I mentioned to you in chapter two, when I first became a dad, I did not feel like I was ready. I had the example of my Dad to help me along, but let's face it, kids don't come with instructions. They take some time to figure out. There is no course in the life stages of being a dad that we have to become certified in before we take the plunge. Early on I knew if I were going to get the hang of this dad thing, I had to surround myself with a team of mentors for advice and counsel. We all need mentors! In fact, you are being mentored here by just reading this book.

Over the years a few of my trusted mentors have shared many golden nuts of wisdom on how to lovingly lead as a father. I'd like to share the top three with you here:

1. **LOVE IN ACTION**. Without question every dad needs to love their kids. Love is the basic foundation on which to build. I have often heard the saying "people don't care how much you know until they know how much you care." I love that saying but I don't think it goes far enough. People only know how much you care by showing them through tangible actions. So for me I've developed the saying "people don't care how much you know, until you show them how much you care." Simply put, lip service just will not do. Love is a verb and is always acting, moving and doing. Kids need love in action constantly.

Keep in mind I am not solely talking about providing a home or gifts here. Kids want and need their dads to show up at their games, recitals, plays, teachers conferences, etc. It shows them that you care and you are by their side. The memory of you being there will leave an indelible mark on their heart that empty words and promises simply cannot do. It takes time to show up for them. Equally important is what it says to them when you cancel appointments or rearrange your schedule to be there for them. They feel like a priority. Love equals time.

2. **LOVE IN WORDS**. We've all heard the childhood nursery rhyme that says, "sticks and stones may break my bones, but words will never hurt me." I hate to break it to you, but words do hurt. Words can break our children's confidence and make them second guess who they are and what they can achieve. Dads should be architects of building our kids up to achieve unlimited possibilities, not tearing them down like a demolition man. Let me give you a cheat sheet. Every kid needs to hear these simple words every day from their dads—I love you, I'm proud of you, I'm here for you, good job and thank you. Don't hold these words hostage from your kids. Lavish them with words of affirmation and support.

3. **LOVE BY ADMITTING WHEN YOU ARE WRONG**. It's often been said that kids don't do what you say, but they do what you do. If we want our kids to tell the truth and take responsibility, we have to set that example by doing the same. I asked a group of kids one day what's the biggest thing about their parents they would change if they

could. To my surprise one kid said, "for my Dad to say I'm sorry when he does wrong." Oh boy it's getting a little uncomfortable now!

One day while we were living in New York City my son did something he was not supposed to do, and I raised my voice to him. I could tell he was dejected by the tone of my voice. I knew then if I did not want him raising his voice to others, I had to do something. I quickly called him to me and said, "Son, that was just not right how I raised my voice at you. I am sorry. It was wrong." His entire demeanor changed. Admitting to our kids that we are not perfect and we sometimes make mistakes is a key lesson in leading in love.

# 4

# FATHERS WHO HEAL

What's really eating away at you? Are regrets consuming your thoughts, so you're forced to shut them down? Can you sit in silence without a mental movie flooding your brain and demanding that you replace the quiet with chaos? How about this one: every time you feel good about life, you start to worry when the other shoe will fall? You're not alone. The pain we carry is tucked away and always available to muck up our lives or turn gold star moments into brown star regrets.

We allow pain, shame and regret to consume us with stress over how to cope with it. Unfortunately, the coping solves nothing. Healing does. Dads, most of us suffer from father wounds. They are traumatic wounds created by the dysfunctional relationship we have or had with our own dad. Most of our challenges today can be traced back to childhood where either a dominant, detached, abusive or absent dad set your path of pain in motion.

Are you carrying the shackles of pain without possibly knowing it? And, if you are aware that something just isn't right, have you developed your own secret way of helping to ease that hurt as opposed to seeking help to heal? If we're not moving toward healing, we're enabling the hurt. The hurt you struggle with today is affecting your child now and potentially into their own adulthood. You can break the cycle.

Can we give you possibly one of the best pieces of advice we've learned?

Time does not heal all wounds.

Trust us, you're not just going to get better, and without an intentional effort at healing an injury, they become exponentially worse. God gives us examples and consequences of how avoiding healing through Him only drags out the suffering. Why do we avoid God? Because the devil whispers in our ear that we're not worthy to be great dads to our kids because we're broken and damaged goods. The father of lies says that we can't trust God the Father because all He wants to do is convict and punish us. Leave Satan's lies in your past. You are created to mirror the one true perfect Father—God.

To progress toward being that perfect dad, you must untether yourself from the baggage of pain or addiction strapped to your back like an unforgiving satchel of doom. We'll tell you that there is no other way than through Jesus Christ the great healer and physician to gain your complete freedom.

Let us share three examples that illustrate how we try and fail to suck it up and deal with our pain instead of turning to God.

## Medication

King David was exalted as a great and mighty ruler. God himself, chose David to be king over Israel because of what He saw on the inside.

> *Man looks at how someone appears on the outside.*
> *But I look at what is in the heart.*
> 1 Samuel 16:7

David's pain was rooted in the rejection by his father, Jessie. His dad never once considered his youngest son David, the lowly shepherd, as being worthy of meeting the prophet Samuel who came on God's direction to anoint a ruler. Yet, there in that rejected, messed-up boy,

Israel had a king. Although David was anointed by God, he didn't come to the throne without serious personal baggage.

David is a lot like us in carrying personal pain from our past. It's like an albatross hanging from our neck and although we might think we're strong enough to carry the burden, we cannot control the rotting stink. We can and must cut the cord to release ourselves from personal pain and experience freedom from the past.

Medicating is a very common but terribly unsuccessful way of dealing with pain. David's medication of choice was the flesh. His sexual addiction caused problems for everyone associated with him. His refusal to heal from his hurt also passed down to his own sons an unholy need for dealing with pain.

How are you medicating what ails you? Are you working yourself to exhaustion just to prove that you can amount to something, or pursuing women to prove that you are lovable, or running your family into debt just to prove that you are able to keep up with the Joneses? Medication takes so many different forms, but they all have the same source—pain. Alcohol, drugs, porn, gambling, suicide ideation, sex, violence or any of the unlimited ways we temporarily satiate will never fill the void created by past injuries. The only permanent solution is God's healing.

David's rejection stung and stuck. Have you been hurt by a parent or someone in your past, and never forgave them? This injury doesn't heal in time, and it's time to forgive and get better.

**Motivation**

The son of King David, Solomon was by far the wealthiest and wisest human ever to grace the earth. Solomon's mother, Bathsheba had come into her marriage with King David as a result of a sordid affair culminating in the murder of her first husband. Because of adultery, her first child conceived with King David died. His father's legacy curse of sexual sin plagued Solomon throughout his life.

Despite his wisdom and close connection to God, he continued to toil in the pain of shame as a result of his own father wound. No, Solomon didn't seek healing from God, he buried himself as most of us do in the pursuits of material achievement for personal affirmation.

Motivation was Solomon's failed attempt to soothe his pain. The more he accumulated things of this world the less he felt deserving. In Ecclesiastes 2 he shares the futility of trying to outwork his hurt. We've included this small section of the scripture, but please read the entire Chapter 2:1-24.

> 10 I denied myself nothing my eyes desired;
> I refused my heart no pleasure.
> My heart took delight in all my labor,
> and this was the reward for all my toil.
> 11 Yet when I surveyed all that my hands had done
> and what I had toiled to achieve,
> everything was meaningless, a chasing after the wind; nothing was gained
> under the sun.
> Ecclesiastes 2:10-11

Are you avoiding the reality that your strained relationship with your child may be attributed to your focus on achieving external approval rather than enjoying their internal love? We can't think of one dad who's lost a relationship with their child who had wished they'd made a little more cash or shot one less stroke on the golf course. Without healing, it will become impossible to fill this empty space. Our spirit requires peace, not prizes.

**Meditation**

Absalom was also King David's son and Solomon's half-brother. His pain, like many with a dominant parent, began at home. Absalom also suffered from intense guilt over doing nothing to defend his sister from a sexual attack by another half-brother. Do you see the generational damages caused by unresolved pain? If your dad hurt you, then chances are your grandfather hurt him. Will you chance continuing the pattern by causing injury to your child? Again, you have the heavenly authority to break the cycle.

Meditation stewed in Absalom's spirit as hatred intensified. For two years he avoided confronting his feelings and the offender before it erupted. Instead of addressing the issue, he killed his brother. Attacks against others is what defines Absalom.

Are you feeling the rage of regret and wrongdoings roil beneath the surface while you look for an outlet to unleash your fury upon? If there is unforgiveness associated with past personal pain, you should understand that avoiding is not winning. You can only sweep so much junk under the rug. Avoiding the truth, no matter how painful it may be, solves nothing. Don't allow lies to fester in your soul.

Which method of satiating past personal pain do you use? Dads, you are good, and you are worthy to be loved. God wants to heal you because He loves you. He's not waiting to smack you around like a carnival game of whack-a-mole. Allow yourself to heal. It's better than the hurt and it will help prevent you from passing down a legacy of suffering to your child.

---

### Scott's Session:

I was suffering. My retirement from law enforcement left me reeling in a world of agony from over 25 years in the only job I'd ever known. Stress, depression, PTSD and addictions that had previously been normalized behind the façade of a high-pressure career, now had no place to hide. I was used to the pain and for years carried suffering around my neck like some noble, masculine badge of honor. It's what we men do, right?

No, we're not meant to suffer. Even worse, my family suffered because of my pain. I at least had the chance to try dealing with my agony or feel the suffocating triggers before it became too dark. My wife and kids on the other hand could only lurk around on eggshells hoping not to become victims of my mood swings and harsh words. They were not meant to suffer either.

Everything came to a head when I confessed to Leah out of a desperate last cry for help. I still recall the words. "When, not if, I kill myself, I'm not going to leave a mess for you or the kids to find." There, I'd said it. My last heroic act on this earth was saving my family the trouble of scraping what was left of me off of a bedroom wall. Although I'd been a fixer and doer all of my career, at that point in my life I couldn't help myself. It was way past my time to seek help for healing. Leah took the lead and got me the counseling I needed to begin the process of becoming whole.

You see, healing is not being weak, it's being smart. God is the great healer for a reason. Jesus focused His ministry on healing for a reason, and the Holy Spirit leads us into atmospheres of healing for a reason. What is that reason? Because you were created by a loving God who wants only what is best for you. What loving father would not want his child to be healthy and whole?

I'll submit that the only way to be healed from the personal pain grounded in either our sin or the sins of others committed against us, is through God the Father. Addictions for example, are symptoms of the pain and not the pain itself. Sure, addictive behavior is painful but the source that became so deeply engrained in your spirit was a consequence of sin. Healing through God the Father is your way to end what it is that has chained you to the past of shame, guilt and failure.

It's also important that our kids learn about pain and healing, so talk to them about it. Appropriate sharing at your kids' maturity comprehension level allows them to witness your humanity. It's an awesome opportunity for them to see that dads do stumble and struggle in life, but we have a loving, merciful and forgiving Father who will always be there to lift us up. Now is the perfect time to get lifted in healing and talk to our kids about it.

### Richard's Session:

It's kinda crazy how this chapter begins and refers to sitting in silence and at peace with yourself. I remember after my father had passed away, I was thinking he would never see me go to prom, graduate high school, get married, see his grandkids, or anything typical of a father or what you have played out over and over in your head.

His death was the catalyst to so many destructive decisions that would begin in my late teenage life. I needed something to heal this overwhelming pain in my soul. Since my father had blamed God for all the misfortune in his life and I pretty much got to see my Dad drink his life away to stave off the pain, I chose to do the same.

This is when the heavy healing—I mean heavy drinking started. When I was intoxicated, the death of my father didn't sting so much. How I wished then I could have said, "Death, where is your sting?" Before my Dad died, I really never drank. I mean I would nurse a beer all night just to be one of the guys but that was it, but the day my Dad died in December of 1981, I tied one on. I was 17 and this was the beginning of something that would affect me till I found a relationship with Jesus and I still had to be delivered.

It was a process that you hear most mature Christians say to trust in.

At night when I went to sleep, I had to blast rock music on my twenty-four-inch speakers. It was so loud that it would shake the walls. Otherwise the silence drove me mad as my mind raced with dark thoughts and despair. Honestly, it didn't take much to rattle the walls. We lived in a tiny two-bedroom home dumped in the poor part of Corpus Christi. I hated that house and everything it represented. I hated my mom and I hated God because it was all His fault. My mom's teachings and my Dad's smack talk created a dysfunction in me that would take decades to undo.

I do still struggle with silence. I have to have something going even when I write, like the TV or a radio. When I sleep, I have two fans going for the noise it makes. I remember going on our first cruise and they took our portable fan because it had a crack in the plastic housing. At night when we were at peace, it was so quiet that I had to open the door to our balcony to hear the waves crashing against the boat. The sound was so peaceful, but the humidity of the salt air was another story.

Funny how the hurt in your life turns you to the thing you vowed you would never do. Mine was alcohol, drugs, pornography, spending, overeating, gambling and all the other vices we can choose to fill our void, our hurts, our disappointments. They are all a false imitation of something that only love can heal and make the change we all so desperately seek.

What is love? Better question is who can truly love? 1st John says, *"God is Love."* So we say, "we don't need God," "we don't need love," "we can do this on our own," and yes, I am guilty of saying this over and over and over. Believing the lie before knowing the truth is something I feel we are all guilty of. If you think about what I just wrote, what I'm actually saying we don't need love because the love we have come to know has hurt most of us deeply. To remove the hurt we want to extinguish that love so it doesn't hurt anymore. Can you see where I'm going with this?

I, like many others, pushed love (God) away from our hearts because we thought love hurt too much. But true love builds, it doesn't destroy. So when we say we don't need love, what we are subconsciously saying is we don't need God, and we start to move away from the one who can heal. This is a vicious cycle indeed.

I even had someone who actually loved me try their best to show me the truth. My late sister knew what I needed to heal even when I didn't. I remember being nineteen years old and three sheets to the wind blasted on alcohol. I was being a jerk and jumping on her bed, but she took out her Bible and waved it at me. "Richie," she called me. "This is all you need." I didn't want to hear anything she had to say because as far as I was concerned, it was all God's fault anyway.

I did not know at the time that Satan was the accuser of the brethren, nor did I know it was Satan's schema to turn me even further away from God and the life He had for me. On a side note: please don't tell yourself, your spouse, your children, your family or your friends that it's God's fault. Whatever you are struggling with is because you're believing a lie that was told to bring desolation of the world and avoid the heeling of your heart. Reject the lie. Live in truth.

*"Heal me, Lord, and I will be healed, see me and I will be saved, for you are the one I praise." And the people all tried to touch him, because power was coming from him and healing them all. "But I will restore you to health and heal your wounds, declare the Lord.*
Jeremiah 30:17

This is where my life really begins. Twenty years later after all the debauchery, I found myself broken, lost and separated. I was nursing the end of a .357 Magnum revolver with the hammer pulled back and my quivering finger on the trigger. I wasn't even praying for God to help me because I didn't know Him.

Of course, God knew me but He just hadn't heard my voice. I'd never once talked to Him. Well, I actually did talk to Him but it was more like screaming and blaming Him for my miserable life. But this time was different. It was the last time I'd shove that pistol barrel in my mouth. I thought for a moment, "This is it; this is what my life had come too." In that moment you really don't think of anyone else because suicide is a selfish death. I was desperately alone, just like I'd been my entire, stinking life. My finger snuggled around the ridged curve of the trigger and I began to apply pressure. Just before the hammer dropped, I heard, "Don't do this."

Although I walked away with my life that day, I still knew that there was walking left to do. I'd lived in spiritual squalor for thirty-nine years and it would require more surrendering on my part to receive the healing to my mind, body and soul I needed to move forward. Part of that daily walk was with my wife, Sheri. At the time we were still dating, she had the deep desire to start attending church. Because I loved her, I went along just to make her happy and to avoid another argument.

What I didn't know was that no matter why I started going to church, God was waiting to show me that He loved me dearly. He loved me as a wounded child, He loved me as a rebellious teenager and yes, He loved me with that pistol between my teeth. It wasn't until I surrendered to His love that I began to heal, and our marriage flourished. Married now for sixteen years, my life is still being healed. I have peace in my life now.

I am not the same person I was many years ago, oh I still have the battle scars, but they are being healed each day by the love of God. Please know it's not easy, but it's simple. When God begins to heal you, it will start a process that begins to heal the world, family and friends around you. All you have to do is ask, He is waiting.

### George's Session:

As men and dads, we all carry around wounds from the past whether we would like to admit it or not. Some of us wear our wounds on our sleeves open for all to see. While others, like me, can hide their wounds and push down the pain thinking nothing can hurt us. As a kid I grew up learning to seemingly let things go and just move on. Like the professional athletes who I currently mentor and coach as an NFL chaplain, I learned to "turn the page" quickly after a loss, bad game or challenging season. Forgetting quickly helped me move on and expect that my best moment or season was just around the corner.

I had gone through almost forty years of life before a childhood wound raised its ugly head. I had watched my father who had only a high school education, work tirelessly serving his congregations as a pastor. The guy worked so hard pastoring one church they eventually gave him twenty churches to oversee at any given time as a district elder. He was excellent at what he did and no one could outwork him. It was not long before he became what some would call a workaholic. He loved what he did primarily because he knew God gave him a gift of pastoring and leading people. But there were other reasons.   Not having much education, my Dad found himself pastoring people who were far more educated and competing for larger churches that had more qualified and educated pastors than he. So, he worked hard at proving himself. We'll come back to proving oneself in just a moment.

While I had an amazing relationship with my father growing up and no major issues, there was at least one moment that affected me more than I ever knew throughout my life. One day when I was a teenager, my father and I were flipping through the TV channels and he came across the nightly weather report. Not knowing I was going to get a spelling bee quiz from my Dad, out of nowhere he asked me to spell "weather." I quickly spelled the word w-h-e-t-h-e-r not knowing which word he was referring to (two very different words pronounced the same but spelled differently). He continued for about five minutes to make me spell the word until I got it right. For him I was spelling it wrong, but I knew I was spelling it right. He scolded me pretty bad for not knowing how to spell a simple word. And if you knew my Dad you had better not try to correct him or it would not go so well.

During those few intense minutes I had taken the bait and the hook was set. It was there that I began my life-long journey of you guessed it, "proving" myself. That moment of feeling inadequate in my Dad's eyes, led me to viewing myself as inadequate in many ways and trying to prove myself to countless people—professors, bosses, friends, congregations, etc. In 2012 it all came to a head as I had just planted a church in New York City, the work capital of the world. I found myself in a major season of burnout. I had gone down the same workaholic path as my father. I was stressed, overworked and trying to prove myself in the city where dreams are made and crushed.

In counseling one day I was asked to trace the beginnings of my thoughts of inadequacy and having to prove myself. I brushed it off and sarcastically thought, *Everyone tries to prove themselves! It's the way of the world.* I had no clue where it had come from until the counselor invited me to simply say the first thing that came to mind no matter how small. It was in that moment I realized I had carried the wound of proving myself from that exchange with my Dad.

Don't get me wrong and think that proving yourself is bad; we live in a results-based world. The point I'm making is those five intense minutes with my father set me on a course of trying to be perfect and showing others that I could do anything. After I identified the wound, I asked God to heal my wounded heart as small as it may seem. I can honestly tell you God our Father has done incredible work in my life since I simply asked him to heal me from my past. Somehow, he lifted the burden and need to prove myself and please others. I've become a better husband, dad, pastor and friend. Thank God for healing the deep things in my soul.

### Juan's Session:

What exactly is healing? Is it what happens after you fall or get physically hurt? You might laugh but I never heard of healing until I got saved. This was a foreign concept for most of my life. I've heard people say out of sight out of mind as a way of stashing their problems aside, but that never worked. All it did was make whatever the pain was even worse. Because I wasn't aware of what spiritual healing meant, I suppressed every feeling deep into the basement of my soul.

Instead of healing from the pain caused by my Dad's abandonment, I shoved hurt and anger deep into my heart. It was like poison and sent me off on a journey to show him that I could make it on my own. Matter of fact, I was determined to be better than he was. Unfortunately being better than him didn't involve grades, promotions or family faithfulness. It meant outdoing my Dad's obsession for drinking, drugs and chasing women.

You only know what you know, right? I didn't even know I was in pain. Because it was the pattern of my life, I assumed that was the way we all felt. I was blind and being led by other blind people. The Bible says in Proverbs 14:12, *"You can rationalize it all you want and justify the path of error you have chosen, but you'll find out in the end that you took the road to destruction."* In some translations it says, *"there's a way that seems right to a man, but it leads you to death."*

It's an internal death that sometimes leads to physical death, Sure, it appears that we are having a good time, but all that laughter will end in heartbreak. I was being led most of twenty-three years by my feelings and without even knowing it, I was numbing my pain from day to day. That's why my kids never got the childhood they deserved. I did not deal with my heart issues, and it bled hurt all over them.

The Bible says in Proverbs 4:23, *"Guard your heart above all else, for it is the source of life."* This is the time where you must come to the cross and exchange your ways for His ways. The cross of Christ is also where you find a body of believers because we can't change alone. God designed for relationships. Healing is a process of accepting and receiving God's word as truth, and its true deliverance where His truth meets our lie.

The truth that we embrace is the reality that we live even if it's a lie. We must accept God's viewpoint and allow His Word to penetrate our spirit because that's the only way to save your soul. Rick Warren says in *The Purpose Driven Life*, that "Change comes from taking risks, and the greatest risk is to be honest with yourself and others." The first step of healing our wounds begins with God. Look within and ask the Holy Spirit right now to search your heart and show you some of the lies you have been living that are destructive to you and your family. Today is your day.

# 5

# FATHERS WHO WALK AWAY

This was a tough chapter to write. We know the stories of kids growing up without a dad and how it affects their lives. Some of us even lived those realities. It hurts and it would've been so much easier to skip this topic instead of tackling it head on. Absent dads have possibly had the single greatest detrimental effect on the American family. That's not an overstatement. If anything, we doubt the actual depth of those harmful effects can ever truly be known, but what we do know is you are an incredibly important part of your family's success and your child's future.

We're going to lay out the facts as reported in a recent United States Census Bureau report because there's not much more we could ever say to better illustrate what baggage gets left behind when the head of the house takes a walk. They are:

- almost 20 million children, or 1 in 4 live without a father in the home.
- kids being 4 times more prone to live in poverty.
- teenaged daughters 7 times more likely to become pregnant.
- kids being more prone to behavioral problems.
- kids facing greater occurrences of abuse and neglect.
- Doubled infant mortality rates.

- high increase of drug and alcohol abuse.
- more likely to go prison.
- twice as likely to suffer obesity.
- increased chances of committing crime.
- two times more prone to drop out of high school.

Our friend, John Finch, author of the book and producer of the documentary, *The Father Effect* adds that children of absent fathers are five times more likely to commit suicide, six times more likely to be institutionalized, eleven times more likely to rape someone and fifteen times more likely to have behavioral disorders. There are so many more dismal demographics, but they're easy enough to search on the internet if these aren't enough to prove men must stand the gap and serve as the spiritual heads of their families. This isn't taking a shot at you or any other man because like we've said, we're imperfect dads too. But what's the disconnect?

Why is there such a dilemma that we can't get it right? It's all so seemingly simple. Man and woman copulate, and a few months later their child is born. Oh look, it's a boy, and he looks like daddy. Proud dad smiles softly as he strokes his calloused palm over the light blue beanie cap the nurse tugged over junior's funnel-shaped head, and dad is overcome with that age-old emotion—panic.

In what would seem like the most naturally occurring relationship in a man's life—it isn't. Fathers and sons (and daughters) are like oil and water. But it wasn't meant to be this way. God's relationship with us was designed to be the blueprint for how we connect with our kids. It was our gift of free will and rebellion that kinda screwed it up.

Men in general stick to a pretty straight forward path as far as the sociology and psychology of man goes. To be honest, we've really not moved the needle very far since Adam. Yeah, that Adam; the first guy and dad. Seriously, it goes that far back. Think we're kidding? Let's take a look.

**The Adam Life**

Are you living the Adam Life? We want to show you that your struggles as a dad didn't begin with you, but the generational challenges faced since the beginning of time can definitely end with you. God the Father created his child Adam for fellowship. The relationship design was perfect as the Father and child enjoyed a seamlessly intimate connection with each other. After all, Adam was created in God's own image.

We are also made in God's image, and just like Adam we have direct access to God the Father. Yep, we also walk with Him and talk with Him and enjoy God's presence in our lives. You even have access to your own Garden of Eden. There's no difference between the Eden that Adam walked in and yours. Let us explain as Eden can become a complicated concept. Historians have searched for the physical garden, which was an actual location on earth.

A translation of the word Eden equals presence, as in God's presence. So, when Adam walked in the garden of Eden, he was walking on earth, with and within God's presence. Does that make sense? Let's take another swing at the piñata. God is omniscient, omnipotent and omnipresent, which means He's twenty-four/seven everywhere, every time. No matter what you do, where you go or what's in your heart, God is there with you—Eden.

Now this is where that gift of free will comes in again. The same thing that caused separation between Adam and the Father is exactly what keeps us at arm's length—sin. While our walk with God can be close in some seasons and distant in others, we always have that deep desire for the Father's love. Your kid has that same desire for God the Father and for you.

Where we relate so closely to Adam is when our relationship with God becomes threatened. Even in the good times of that relationship we are still faced with the reality of free will. And despite our love for Him just as Adam loved Him, when the chips are on the table and we have an opportunity to show our love for Him through obedience by fleeing from sin, we instead sometimes bite the apple. Some of us might have bitten that apple a lot. And often.

This is where the complexity of father and child relationships origi-nated. Adam's sin created the break in their bond and without a path for reconciliation, the close connection eroded. Not only did rebellious behavior effect Adam's relationship with his Father, but it created a faithless environment for raising his two sons, Cain and Abel. Of course, as you know, Cain killed Abel and was then also separated from a relationship with his dad, Adam. Ultimately, Adam's negative behavior has led up to where we are today.

## Sin

Sin separated Adam from the close relationship with his Father. Our Father wants to bless us with more than our natural minds can imagine. Yet we're so afraid. Yes, we said the "A" word. Too often, we'd rather skid through the muck of what life allows than grab the glory that God is bursting to bestow upon us. We allow our sin to go unrepentant and unforgiven until it exiles us just like Adam from the Garden of Eden and Cain separated from his family.

We're not blasting Adam or any other the biblical heroes we'll discuss, but it's important for you to see that those who stood tallest had to first be picked up off their behinds. God didn't stick with them because of their misdeeds, but because He knew the desires of their hearts and potential to be incredible dads.

## Did Adam Doom Us?

That's a fair question, and if you choose to live under the action of the first Adam, then yes, you're pretty much a stuck duck. Why? Because nothing you can do, no amount of money you can pay or weight you can overhead press is ever going to be good enough to earn your way back into God's good graces. Why? Because God gave you the way back—Jesus.

Dad, you're not doomed. Even if your life up to this very moment has been junk, it doesn't have to continue to be so. Our past isn't there to define us, it's there to remind us. If you've lost connections with your child or haven't remained consistent with custody visitations or whatever has strained or severed that relationship, you can experience restoration. But it all starts with renewing the God connection. So, you have a choice to make. Adam didn't have the same choice you now have thanks to Jesus.

Will you remove the barrier of sin that has created separation from God so that He may work in your life to restore or improve the bonds with your child? We cannot expect to improve our dad game by avoiding the example from the one perfect Father. It cost you nothing to receive His gift that helps pave the path to renewal. Ephesians 2:8-9 makes it pretty clear that grace is God's gift. Will you receive it, or continue crawling through the pain, disappointment and darkness from of failing to be the dad you know you were meant to be? Choose wisely!

## Bigger Better Deal

We've been picking on Adam harder than a freshman at a frat rush party. He was *el numero uno*. He had no student loans, no baby mommas, no slow Wi-Fi or worries about next year's fantasy football picks. This guy was God's "plus one," and he was the very first global CEO. Seriously, the guy had it all.

But, just like us, he wanted more. Adam wanted the bigger, better deal. Whether it's making more money, the latest sports car or the first-six-months-free cable packages, we want more. So did Adam, and we're still paying for his selfish power grab back in the garden.

Adam spoke directly with God, and yet he still fumbled. We also have direct access to God, but we too find ways to drop the ball. If we're willing to listen, you'll hear God speak as clearly to you as He did with Adam. When the word gets fuzzy it's because you started adding filters to the listening process. God told His number one boy to enjoy everything in paradise. So, God put Adam in the garden to work it, and to keep it up so that he could enjoy the fruits of his labor.

Then He very clearly told Adam that it was okay to eat from any tree in the garden except for one very specific tree. As much as God loved Adam, He made no bones about it, and if His main man ate from that one tree, he'd die. Check out Genesis 2:15-17 for reference. There are boundaries in fatherhood and consequences for violating them. If you've been guilty of operating beyond the guardrails of mature, nurturing dad behavior, then a strained or lost relationship with your child might just be the price you both are paying.

Instead of throwing stones at our very first alpha dad, how about instead we accept that we've not progressed far from where Adam was in the days of Eden. Look, sin is sin. Adam bit a piece of fruit, and his son Cain murdered his brother, Abel. Both sins resulted in exile and separation from God (spiritual death).

So how about us, men? What's your sin? Adultery, porn, alcohol, drugs, violence, greed, lust, pride, theft, covetousness, refusing to forgive others, your dad, your child or yourself? You see, Dad, we do walk with God. We have His direct Word of instruction, and yet still, we bite what is forbidden. But no worries, like we said, you have the God-ordained authority to break those chains to past bad dad behavior and chart a new course for your family.

### Richard's Session:

Scott already mentioned this was a hard chapter to write and brother he was not kidding. After I wrote that sentence, I literally sat for a while and thought about how tough it was for me losing my father when I was only seventeen. As I rapidly approached manhood, I needed those talks with my Dad. Before he died, I'd always dreamed of having the man-to-man relationship with my Dad, but his self-destructive behavior and premature death ended even the most remote possibility of him guiding me through that difficult stage in my life. I still long for even having had one of those talks.

My friends were great, and their dads even tried having those "What it means to be a man" talks with me. Unfortunately, I was so hemmed up with hate and anger over losing my Dad that I wanted nothing to do with theirs. I know it might sound odd, but even today when I'm alone I pretend he's with me as I imagine asking him the questions that haunted me for decades. Man, how different my life might've been had I been able to ask him:

"Dad, I have friends who are wanting me to smoke pot, what do you think?"; "Dad, what do you think about sex before marriage or even dating?"; "How do I know if she is the right woman for me?"; "Dad, what do you see as weaknesses in me and what about strengths?";

"Dad, what do I need to watch out for as I get older?"; "Dad what about saving money?"; "Dad, can you watch your grandkids today?"

The real questions would be "Dad, why did you drink so much all the time?"; "Dad, why are you using alcohol to deaden the pain?"; "Dad, are you drinking because of me?"

Do any of these sound familiar? Maybe you actually got to ask your dad these questions and more, or maybe it's not too late. Guess what? If your kids haven't asked them of you, maybe you can help them start that conversation right now. Too many of us still carry the weight of never having enjoyed the memory of a single boy-to-man conversation with our dad, But thanks to having accepted Jesus into my life, He is the answer to all of my questions and more. He will be there for you too.

*So you will become sons of your Heavenly Father, for He makes his sun rise*
*for sinner and saints and sends rain among the unjust and just.*
Matthew 5:45

You see God helps the motherless and the fatherless but if we've never been taught this we rest upon our human thoughts and processes on how life keeps dealing us losing hands. There was a time before knowing God that I used to say if it weren't for bad luck, I'd have no luck at all. Nothing good ever happened to me. Even without God in my life, I was living out of the Bible and didn't know it.

I know it's a little screwy sounding, so let me explain. Proverbs 18:21 says, *"The power of life and death are in the power of the tongue."* I was saying with my mouth everything that was happening to me. Years and years of living with a black cloud over me and to know now that I was causing it. It wasn't bad luck, it was bad speech. I was bringing all these bad things to life, which was bringing death to my soul.

As Christian men we have to do a better job reaching those around us. I can say because my father was not there for me that I started making bad choices and decisions one right after another. Every time you speak you plant seeds in life. Those seeds will bring a harvest. Whether what's reaped is good or bad depends on what seeds you first sowed. We can also easily fall into a destructive cycle of repeating the habits of negative thinking and speaking.

When we make bad decisions, we start to form a habit of repeating these same choices. It happens so easily that we're not really aware of what it is we're doing to ourselves. The beauty of God's Word is that once we start making good choices, it feels funny because you're not accustom to it yet. You can and will grow used to it and eventually expect what you speak power into.

I look back now after fifteen plus years in ministry and see that we still have uncomfortable things happen but for the most part we are surrounded by really good things. We see it each day, and not just with us but everyone around us. There is no other way. We have to live our life for Christ and let Him help us with serving Him to make the right choices in life that will glorify His holy name. This all starts and stops with how we choose our attitude. Choose wisely.

The beauty of God the Father is that even if you are negative, He still loves you and will never abandon you. Of course, that's not true for many men as dads or who had dads who walked away. Circumstances vary widely, but the pain is all very similar and real. What about those of us dads who didn't walk with God? If we never understood that Jesus wants a relationship with us and not religion, we might miss the free gift of a life with Him. We might suffer consequences simple because we didn't pursue the perfect Father.

I was so far from being a perfect father, and I do love my kids, but that wasn't enough to prevent them from being hurt. There is nothing— and when I say nothing, I mean nothing—that I wouldn't do for them. You know when you know in your knower that your life is kind of jacked up and your children have been hurt by you and your bad choices? You can feel that they have paid a price they never should've had to pay. My imperfection outside of Christ tallied a heavy price on my kids despite my love for them.

Being jacked up meant not understanding that I was the one causing their pain and I had the power to stop making stupid choices that caused them serious consequences. I even recall thinking that it was the church's job to fix my kids. All I had to do was get them there and it'd all be taken care of. I was wrong. Church can teach them the things in life that they need, that will help them, that will change their life, but fixing the source of what was messing up their lives was my responsibility because I was the cause.

You see, I didn't want my kids to go through what I'd gone through as a child. It was horrible for me and continued to hurt me, so why would I want them to experience even the slightest agony? What I did wasn't protecting them from pain, I was actually creating a destructive environment at home that at times was equal to or worse than what I'd gone through. I antagonized my kids to a point that they walked away and wanted nothing to do with me. This shattered my heart.

*Fathers, do not provoke or irritate or exasperate your children with demands that are trivial or unreasonable; nor by favoritism or indifference; treat them tenderly with loving kindness so they will not lose heart and become discouraged or unmotivated with their spirit broken.*
Colossians 3:21

Sometimes, we dads walk away, and sometimes our kids walk away from us because of us. We can want it so badly that all we make happen is bad. I was so on fire for Christ that I wanted my kids to feel that same sense of connection. I pushed God on them and almost demanded that they get to the point where I was in my faith walk. My heart was in the right place, but my lack of knowledge on how to treat my little ones was way off. It's not our job to save others. That's for God. Instead of showing them the unconditional love that God showed me, I was busy trying to force religion down their throats.

Looking back, I can totally understand why they walked away. I wish now I would've simply listened to them, but I was too busy telling them what to do. Oddly enough, that's the very same thing my Dad did to me. Dad, we have to intentionally work to build and maintain relationships with our kids. Just because we wear the name plate that reads, Dad, doesn't mean the connection grows without effort. Rules without relationship equals rebellion. Kinda like our relationship with our Heavenly Father. If you want to be a dad who doesn't walk away or force your kids not to walk away from you, mirror God the perfect Father.

The other authors and I believe in you! It's not too late to forgive yourself and forgive anyone else you need to so you can begin to move forward. If things are bad right now, speak life into your circumstance and turn things around. Forgiving is power, and we'll talk about what forgiveness and what it really means in the next chapter.

**George's Session:**

While I don't know personally what it is like to feel the effects of an absent dad or a father who walked away, I've seen the effects it brings into the lives of many. Many of my childhood friends did not have fathers who were present in their lives and I could see how they longed to have a relationship with their father much like I had with mine. It's heartbreaking as all kids desire to have their father active in their lives.

My kids, Jay and Camryn, did not always like me being the protective dad, the disciplinarian or the dad who showered them with "I love you" or "I'm proud of you." In fact, one day my daughter expressed I did not have to say it as often as I did because she knew I loved her and was proud of her based on how often I told her. I often encouraged them not to take it for granted that they had a present dad, that yes, sometimes went a little overboard, but I only wanted the very best for them. A year into my son's freshman year of college he called and graciously began to thank me for being there for him as a dad and always loving him. You see, all throughout his first year he met class-mates who did not have a relationship with their dad and he had seen firsthand how it affected them.

Sadly, my lovely wife, who is an incredible mom, wife and friend, did not grow up with her biological dad. In fact, she has never seen him a day in her life. It's something still to this day that I cannot believe because he's out there somewhere. For nearly fifty years he has been MIA. He simply created a child and somehow abandoned the responsi-bility and stewardship that comes along with what it means to a real dad. All children desire to know what it's like to have a present dad for protection, provision, stability and consistency. A dad that gives them the ability to feel safe and secure. A dad that helps shape their identity, value and sense of self-worth.

Over the years my wife has not really spoken much about her dad. She's done well at getting the inner healing that she needed to not allow it to affect our marriage and children much. When we were first married, I often thought that him not being around was his loss. But then as our kids got a little older and put two and two together, they realized that he had abandoned them too. No calls, cards, visits or anything. Dads who chose to walk away unfortunately leave a wake of questions, emotions and realities that can affect generation after generation.

As a husband and dad, I had to decide earlier on that his unfortunate egregious abandonment would not derail our new family and our future. Sure, in the beginning I had to deal with my wife's issues of not trusting men and her feeling like I could walk out on her at any moment. There were times when her independent nature and her closely guarding her heart made it difficult to build a healthy marriage. It was tough. Yet I realized her hard exterior was just a way to guard against getting hurt and being abandoned again.

For the last twenty-five years, I've tried to be not only the best husband and father but also an example of God's redemption story of healing and restoration. Over the years my wife has in her own way thanked me for being a part of her healing process. Not because I have any magical power but simply because I was man enough not to walk away when times got tough. Ironically, the way I've loved and cared for my kids and her has helped her see men in a whole new light. As dads, our presence and example are a part of God's redemptive story.

### Juan's Session:

Wow, this book keeps challenging me to dig deeper into my reality, and I'll admit that I've cried a lot because the truth of me walking away from my children hurts. I believe it's important for me to share with you because the only way we're going to up our dad game is to face whatever it is we did or didn't do as dad so we can make it right from this day forward.

The old saying, "the apple doesn't fall far from the tree," is not just a saying. There's some truth to that. As I talked about in an earlier chapter, my Dad, who had offered me a chance to live with him if I got cleaned up, yanked the rug out from under me right before I got out of rehab. He'd found another new and soon-to-be ex-girlfriend who'd moved into his revolving door life and he decided she was more important than the many broken promises he'd made to me.

That disappointment crushed me more than most of the others because this was my first real offer to live with my Daddy. Even as a young man I still needed him, and I was so pumped up at the thought of moving in with him to prove that I was a man in his eyes and not just some junkie. What his rejection created was an inner vow-based emotion that led me straight into destruction whenever things got difficult.

"I'll show you" became my motto based on anger and rage aimed at a Dad who walked away from my life one time too many. The experience taught me to also walk away instead of standing my ground or keeping my promises when times got too tough. Rather than dealing with the reality of the situation, I'd walk away to get numb with sex or drugs.

I walked away from my first marriage because I was clueless. I was man enough to impregnate her but not so much as to take care of them or myself. I knew nothing about leading my family because I'd never been led in my life. It was everyone for themselves. All I knew was once things got hard, it was time to walk away or find an easier time. Guess what? I also walked away from my second marriage because I was trapped in a dysfunctional cycle. Unless you change you, every relationship will start and stop the same way. The difference is you.

Generational cycles are real and Dad, you have the power to break that curse. I have forgiven my Dad because he only did what he knew to do by walking away. It isn't right, but the only way something will change is if we change. It starts with the way we think. We become what we behold because whatever we look up to is what we become. My Dad set his sights on easier times, and I did the same thing. Until I changed my focus, of course.

I broke that toxic behavior of walking away once I encountered a love that never abandoned me. The love of God the Father is never-ending and taught me what it looked like to remain engaged and refuse to walk away. I learned to love because God first loved me.

Tom Lane of Gateway Church said, "We often make short sighted decisions because it is difficult for us to consider long term benefits of sacrificial investment in the lives of our children." Dad, if you are distracted and unfocused where your child is concerned, commit to spending the time with them. You are a very important part of their life, so don't miss the opportunity and don't walk away.

### Scott's Session:

I'm going to take a deep plunge on this one because it's very painful for me. Honestly, I spent time praying about whether or not to share, but God unmistakably said, "Do it." Back in the eighties, yes that far back, I was running and gunning and completely addicted to my career as an undercover narcotics agent. My obsession with living a double life didn't switch off once I left my latest assignment and I strolled back home. I recall one of the last things my wife yelled before it all imploded was that I'd become just like them. She was right. I'd become one of the monsters I hunted. It was no surprise that my first marriage ended, and within months, I was back on the set looking for someone to fill the painfully empty space.

I was a mess, and after a brief month and a half marriage, my second wife left and returned to her home in Puerto Rico. It was a chaotic rebound and one would've thought, with our marriage ending after less than two months, there'd be no harm, no foul. Except she was pregnant.

I saw my son twice. The feeble attempts to communicate pre-facetime with a toddler who spoke Spanish dead-ended with my despair over the frequent yelling matches with his mother. Before he could hold the phone for himself and learn a few English words, I'd walked away from even trying to continue a connection. I rationalized that he was better off without me and that if his mother remarried, then he'd get a dad and I'd be off the paternal hook.

Except that he wanted his dad.

He's in his twenties as I write this, and there's rarely been a day I haven't thought about him and hurt because I just didn't know what to do. I failed at appeasing myself that he was better off without me; I knew better. I know the data for boys without a dad in their lives, but what was I to do? Was I supposed to reach out to him or his mother to start something that never was?

In 2019, God spoke to me with a crystal-clear conviction. He recounted my unbridled youth of living in destructive sin. Between the high-octane danger addiction to my job and the effects of past personal pain, I'd caused major damage to a lot of people who'd stumbled into my path. The habit of blaming my ex-wives for our failed marriages had hit a brick wall. Sure, I'd prayed for God to forgive me years ago, but I'd never taken personal responsibility for my actions. In that 2019 conviction, God told me to write a letter to both of my ex-wives and claim responsibility for my behavior. It was an incredible revelation to write an apology letter after more than twenty years, and I knew it was the right thing to do.

Except I didn't.

In 2020, God gave me the direction to write this book. He also told me to co-author it with Richard, Juan and George. I didn't question why because I love these men and was excited to invite them to share the journey. So with my cohort of writers, I began bashing the keyboard. I knew I'd complete my assigned task in no time, but something had my mind so distracted that I'd stopped writing all together. Conviction had overcome creativity.

I shared the story of God's instructions for writing the letters to my ex-wives with Juan. I also shared with him my failed relationship with my son. As a pastor, his heart was evident, but he didn't hesitate to call me out on why I hadn't obeyed God by writing the letters. It was pride, ego and probably a million other stupid excuses that kept me from alignment with God the Father. The more I explained the past to Juan, the more certain I was he'd see my side of the argument.

Except he didn't.

About mid-2020, Juan was in Puerto Rico on business and pleasure. The first day he called to talk about the book we were co-writing, he said, "You're putting this project in jeopardy. God's not going to let you write this book about fatherhood because you're a hypocrite." Honestly, I was mad and wasn't sure I wanted to continue the phone call or write the book. I knew he was speaking the truth out of love, but I sure wasn't in the mood to be called a hypocrite. My heart grew hard against Juan, the book and writing the letters.

Two days later Juan and I were back on the phone, except I wasn't as happy to hear his voice. He was talking about how gorgeous the beaches were in San Juan and I was thinking about the reality that his eyes were seeing the very same sights my son's eyes had seen while growing up on the same island. Then Juan, who is also Puerto Rican asked, "Why didn't you fight for your son?" I was stunned; fight for him? I muttered something about the hard times I was going through back then. I'd hoped that would throw him off my trail, but he persisted.

"Dad, I'm your Puerto Rican son. Why didn't you fight for me?" Juan asked.

I was stunned. I heard what I thought to be my son's voice coming across the phone from my pastor and friend, Juan. I couldn't speak as tears rivered over my face. I'd never thought about it as having not been willing to fight for a relationship. I incorrectly assumed surrendering my role as dad was the best course of action. I was wrong. I knew how hard that had to have been for Juan to confront me with the truth but having struggled with his own dad walking off and the damage it caused in his life showed just how deep his love ran for me and the son I never knew.

God the perfect Father had perfectly orchestrated that phone call from Juan. My friend hadn't returned to Puerto Rico just for business and pleasure. He'd returned to make amends and right wrongs that left him estranged from many back in his former home. It was God who set the circumstances to convict me of my sin of willful disobedience to writing the letters and taking personal responsibility for my awful actions over two decades earlier. I promised Juan I'd write those letters the next day.

Except that I wrote them right then.

Oh how I wish I could tell you that as of this book being published, my son and I have reconciled and are on the path to growing a positive relationship. The truth is, I have no idea whether the letters were ever read. I've continued to pray for reconciliation and am better prepared to receive the gift of a restored relationship because I was first able to admit my faults, ask forgiveness and accept that I was the source of my own bad choices. It's been almost a year since I mailed them and as of early into 2021, still no word. It would be easy to wave the white flag of surrender and stop praying for reconciliation with my son.

Except that I won't.

# 6

# FATHERS WHO FORGIVE

"But you don't know what they did to hurt me."

Yes, we do because we've all been hurt by other people. To be completely honest, we've also caused other people to be hurt, so yes, we do know, and this is why we want to hang out a bit and talk about forgiving.

Forgiving is kinda like a really big deal. Why? Because of our sin nature, we're all doomed. Actually because of our sin we deserved nothing short of death (Romans 6:23). But God, the sacrificially loving example of how to be a nurturing dad, forgave us so that we might continue in a relationship with Him and come to know a blessed life as we've never experienced before.

Let's take an even deeper look at the extent of forgiveness God was willing to offer into our lives. He loved us so much that He gave his only begotten Son as a sacrificial atonement of our sins so we may be forgiven of those same transgressions that keep us away from Him. Forgiveness is an ultimate act of freedom that we are afforded because God loved us and forgave us first.

Even His precious son, Jesus Christ, as he hung agonizing on that wooden cross, looked at the very same people who crucified him and said, *"Father, forgive them, for they do not know what they are doing."* (Luke

23:34 NIV). Could you imagine after being beaten, flogged, mocked, and rejected by those closest to you, that you would have a speck of compassion to forgive them for what they did to you as you hang dying? None of us would, and that's why it was Jesus who gave himself as that sacrifice so we can know forgiveness.

Dad, God is so serious about the act of forgiving that he clearly tells us if we do not forgive others, He will not forgive us for our own sins. Now to put that in perspective, there's only one sin that is absolutely unforgivable, and it's blaspheming the Holy Spirit (Mark 3:28-29). Therefore, by willful refusal to forgive someone else, you're intentionally placing yourself separate and apart from the grace of forgiveness and the blessings of God by condemning yourself into the same isolated supernatural status as the unforgiven blasphemers of the Holy Spirit.

> *For if you forgive others their trespasses, your heavenly Father will also forgive you. But if you do not forgive others, then your Father will not forgive your trespasses.*
> Matthew 6:14-16

Now that's serious business and if it's not enough of an incentive to learn to forgive, then we're not sure there's anything else we could do to convince you. But we won't give up trying!

## Men Struggle

Most men struggle with forgiveness because we're under the impression that forgiving someone lets the other person off the hook for what they did to hurt us. We're also afraid forgiving will make us look weak, so instead we get amped up in the fantasy of getting even or an upper hand through revenge. It's easy to continue harboring hard feelings against someone who hurt us, but that anger is like poison we ingest while trying to hurt someone else. No grudge held was worth so much as to separate us from God.

But forgiveness isn't for the violator's benefit, it's for ours. Forgiving frees us from the hurt and the hurter. Dad, you must take the lead in forgiving. God our Father showed us how to do it and why it must be done. Unforgiveness is your jailer. It's sort of a pain prison where the ones we refuse to forgive are our captors. They tug the chain, and we feel the pain. We can cut that invisible cord right this second like a hot supernatural K-BAR knife slicing through soft butter by forgiving them.

## Soul Ties

Let's step right into a big steaming pile of none of our business. Do you need to forgive your dad? Oh, did that hurt you like it hurt us the first time we realized we needed to forgive our own dads? Why haven't you? If you're like most of us, there are deep wounds called soul ties created by our relationship with our dad. Some soul ties are positive memories, while others are negative and destructive to you. Those that hurt and harmed you, if left unforgiven, will aggressively manifest into behavioral influencers. Don't misunderstand the negative power of unforgiving. It does cause pain and can lead to physical illnesses and emotional misery.

If there are others to forgive, and there probably are, then you should work your way around the room, but let's start with what you most identify with—Dad. Forgiving him is your first and most important mission. If they are still alive, most of them continue suffering in silence and regret for things they did or didn't do with you. Forgiving them also establishes the example of honoring your dad as God commanded in Deuteronomy 5:16 (Ten Commandments) and allows you a glimpse of the powerful effect forgiving has over men's lives. If your dad has passed away or there are extenuating circumstances preventing you from communicating with him, there is still forgiveness to be given.

Remember, forgiving is for you, not them. Actually, you don't even have to tell them that you forgive them. God needs you to clear your heart so He can occupy it with a greater capacity to love and, of course, forgive.

While we're on the topic of dads and forgiving, let's not overlook that you may have hurt your own kid. It may not have been intentional, and you probably didn't even realize it happened, but this is also a great time to talk to them about the liberation of forgiveness. While you're at it, ask your kids if there is any offense you caused and ask them to forgive you. We don't want to shackle our own kids down by unforgiveness, and again, it's the perfect way to lead by example.

## Pulling A Fast One

Do you recall when Peter thought he'd pull a fast one over on Jesus by asking about only forgiving seven times? Yeah, Peter went off on his own a time or two just like we do, but Jesus quickly corrected him that we are to forgive seventy times seven. That doesn't mean four hundred and ninety times and then they're condemned. Jewish tradition called for you to forgive someone three times. Peter decided to play it safe when questioning Jesus about forgiving others by adding an additional three times and for the sake of being extra religious, he added one more to grow on. Can you see why Jesus had to rebuke Peter so often? But seriously, His command to forgive seventy times seven was equal to infinity. This leads us to our next topic, and we promise it's not math.

We talked about the wounds you may have endured by your own dad, or an adult male in your life, but let's not forget about those smaller humans living rent free in our homes. Our kids are so dear to us that their words and actions have the potential to pierce our heart and our pride faster than any keyboard gorilla on social media. And yes, it's okay to feel betrayal or hurt because of them. You might even graduate to an occasional feeling of anger, but don't let that make you carry guilt about it either. God experiences anger and paraphrasing Ephesians 4:26, anger is not a sin as long as you don't sin in your anger. But what you must do is forgive them, and if your kid is anything like our kids, you'll have to forgive them a lot. Like, a whole lot.

## God Got It

Dad, whether we are forgiving our own folks, our kids or someone who said something stupid a year ago, it's an ongoing process that does not come easily. But, just like anything else, the more you work at it, the better you'll become. You will not believe the calm and clarity it'll give you once you're not wrapped up in emotional reactions to everything that blows across your path. Peace and freedom allow you to respond on your own terms and in your own time without anyone else owning a piece of who you are.

Okay, are you still on the fence about forgiving seeming a little too passive? We understand and want to assure you that active forgiveness is anything but passive. You are moving heaven and earth with your prayers, but if you're still shackled to your offending jailer, then those potentially powerful prayers aren't getting past the ceiling.

Can you imagine praying for your sweet child yet knowing those very petitions to God hold no authority because there is unforgiveness in your life? We're not trying to guilt you, but without the whole truth, you might head off in the wrong direction.

Another truth bomb we're going to drop on you is the second part of being forgiven of your own sins. Not only does God want you to forgive your offender, but He also wants you to bless them as well. Tough, we know, but here are two tips for knowing if you've truly forgiven someone or not:

1. You've stopped talking about what it was they did to hurt you, and
2. The anger or hate in your heart is gone and you are able to pray for their blessings.

Yeah, but…

We know what's coming, so we waited to the end of this section to give you incentive. When someone sins, their actions are a spiritual offense, and not even the FBI has jurisdiction over that. Only God has control over the supernatural, so it's His responsibility to take action against the sinner.

*"Avenge not yourselves, beloved, but give place unto the wrath of God: for it is written, Vengeance belongeth unto me; I will recompense, saith the Lord."*
Romans 12:19

You see, God will take vengeance on the offender, but He cannot get started as long as you are in the way through your unforgiveness. Once you free yourself, then God is free to act. Now we know you might be hoping for some Old Testament smiting, but what God decides to do with the offender is His decision alone. Remember, we've all sinned and fallen short of the glory of God. That means He chose to love you as He loves those who you have forgiven. Besides, who would you rather have taking care of those who enjoy making others miserable than God himself?

---

### George's Session:

Growing up my parents tried to model their marriage and build our family off biblical principles and God's word. Sure we did not have a perfect family, as there were plenty of moments of intense fellowship (that is a faith spin on fights), contention and breakdowns. Every family has them from time to time, some more than others. However, one of the principles that my mother and father tried to instill into our family dynamic was the ability to move on after wrongdoings and disagreements. More specifically they taught us how to move on through the biblical lens of forgiveness. By the time I graduated from college and moved out on my own, my father became a professional at forgiveness as I gave him plenty of exercise and things to forgive.

As an influential pastor and leader, my Dad would often let us know as kids that the way we conducted ourselves outside of the house was a direct reflection on him in the eyes of the larger community and church world. He would often say, *"Don't make me look bad by your youthful actions."* I wish I could tell you I never made him look bad. Unfortunately, as the youngest of three I think I tested his wishes more than my siblings.

On not just one but three different occasions, I had to make a call to my father to come down to the county jail and kindly bail me out. Now I know what you are thinking—not you George! Yelp, I did. Don't judge me though, as it took me some time to get to where I am today. Every time I made a call from the county jail, I knew he would be disappointed and hurt like any parent would. I knew he would be left trying to rationalize how it would look to the community and in the eyes of church members.

I desperately hated each time I had to call but I was so thankful I had a faithful father to turn to in my moments of maturing and finding myself. You see each time he showed up, bailed me out and picked me up was a picture of our perfect heavenly father's grace in all of our lives. There is a sermon in there that we are all benefactors of God showing up, bailing us out and picking us up when we needed him the most.

My father not one time left me there to figure life out on my own. He never let his reputation as a pastor in the community get in the way of his responsibility as a father to show love and forgiveness to his son even when it hurt. Not once did he suggest my ways were irredeemable or unrepairable. Don't get me wrong, he gave me a stern talking to each time, but after that he would always wrap his loving arms around me and say, *"Let's go home."*

As a son and now father, I will never forget his patience for forgiving me and believing my best was yet to come. We all need the example of a loving and forgiving father. Better yet we all need to *be* the example of a loving and forgiving father.

### Juan's Session:

"I forgive you."

There, that was easy enough for getting out of a jam or getting you out of my face. Isn't that what we think forgiveness involves? Unfortunately, as powerful as the act of true forgiveness is, it's often misunderstood and misused. If we say we're sorry but fail to change the behavior that caused the offense, then that's manipulation to ask forgiveness without follow-through.

Honestly, I always thought forgiveness meant saying, "I'm sorry," and then moving along. Because I failed to understand what forgiving someone actually meant, I'd lie to them that they were forgiven when they apologized, but I'd make sure they'd suffer for having hurt me. I'd rage on by planning their big payback in revenge for disrespecting me.

. . .

I wasn't open to forgiving or being forgiven because I'd created defensive personalities to guard myself against any emotion. Before I grounded my identity in Jesus Christ, I used different aliases to create a false identity of being tough so no one could ever hurt me. Because I was living only for myself and not for God, I thought forgiveness was for the weak. It wasn't until I experienced God's grace that I was able to show grace to others.

Understanding that had God not allowed His son to die for me on the cross, I would spend my eternity in hell finally made me realize that, by plotting revenge instead of offering forgiveness, I was in fact living my hell on earth. I was a prisoner to my own rage and refusal to forgive. It all had to begin with forgiving the person who hurt me first, often and most deeply, my Dad.

Did he deserve to be forgiven? Did I? Do you? The truth is none of us deserve God's grace, but that's what makes it such a beautiful gift of love. It's unearned and undeserved. Once we learn to forgive others in love and grace, we also experience God's forgiving nature that first led Him to show us grace. If you're like me and learn better from real-life examples, let me show you this illustration of true forgiveness.

As God's son hung agonizing on that wooden cross, He looked at the very same people who crucified him and said, *"Father, forgive them, for they do not know what they are doing."* (Luke 23:34 NIV).

Did the very people who nailed Him to that cross deserve to be forgiven for putting Him there? Of course not, but in His loving nature as God, he gave them the gift of forgiveness as opposed to plotting revenge. We must do the very same thing by forgiving no matter what our emotions tell us.

When you have experienced grace and you know you have been forgiven, you are more gracious and forgiving to others. Allow me to close this section of my witness with this verse from the Book of Romans 15:1-5 (Passion translation)

*Now, those who are mature in their faith can easily be recognized, for they don't live to please themselves but have learned to patiently embrace others in their immaturity. Our goal must be to empower others to do what is right and good for them, and to bring them into spiritual maturity. For not even the*

*most powerful one of all, the Anointed One, lived to please himself. His life*
*fulfilled the Scripture that says:*

*All the insults of those who insulted you fall upon me.*

*Whatever was written beforehand is meant to instruct us in how to live. The*
*Scriptures impart to us encouragement and inspiration so that we can live in*
*hope and endure all things. Now may God, the source of great endurance and*
*comfort, grace you with unity among yourselves, which flows from your rela-*
*tionship with Jesus, the Anointed One.*

**Scott's Session:**

Forgiveness is a funny thing. I don't mean funny ha, ha. I mean that if
we don't forgive, it's going to get funny in a bad way. God the Father
doesn't mince words when it comes to forgiving one another because
it's the reason His son was crucified.

Most dads picture the act of forgiving as some grand finale in a
coming-of-age movie. The truth is, forgiveness can be as world
changing as Jesus dying on the cross so that we all can know the
atoning forgiveness of our sins, to the self-whisper in your prayer
closet because someone at work made you angry.

I think because we get knocked around sometimes, immediately a
topic like being forgiven sends red flags to dad that we've messed up
or hurt someone. That may be true, but there are many times where
we're the ones having to forgive someone else. One of the people we
rarely consider having to forgive is our kids. You mean those perfect
little angels? They might be the apple of our eye, but they are human
and when they say or do something that stings our spirit, we must
realize that even they must be forgiven.

We all sin and fall short of the glory of God, and although we may not
want to even consider it, that also means our kids. I'm not saying
they're bad people, but they are not above the divine nature of God. As
men, we usually suck it up and move on, but in the cases where the
offenses are beyond the stage of simple misunderstandings and graduate to willful disobedience or intentional harm, forgiveness is
required.

I'd say the majority of time it's going to be you taking the initiative to forgive them whether they know you have or not. They probably aren't aware they hurt you or just don't know how to approach you to ask for forgiveness. This is an awesome opportunity for you to teach your child about the power of forgiving. If you haven't shown them a real-life example of asking for forgiveness, now's the time.

Personally, I've wasted time trying to let their hurts roll off my back. I thought it was unmanly to admit to my child that they'd hurt my feelings. Eventually, pain will manifest itself and what I thought was no big deal might end up causing resentment toward my very own child. Not forgiving our kids causes us both to lose. We know what God says about forgiving others of their sins and we also know that unless we teach our kids about forgiveness they may never learn.

Fathers who forgive their kids reduce the potential for developing hard feelings toward them, whether they realize it or not, as well as allowing them to enjoy the blessings of being forgiven. Forgive, ask for forgiveness and teach you kids the reality of what to do when they've offended others or have been offended. Freedom from the hurt is as close as the gift of forgiveness.

### Richard's Session:

My Dad taught me something super special when I was just a tot. What he had to share was very important to him because he always made sure I'd remember what he said. He claimed it would get me through life no matter what anyone else tried to tell me. The first time he shared this, I was so excited because he'd actually sat me down to talk to me. That alone was rare and weird, but I sensed there was something magic in what he wanted to say.

*"Son,"* my Dad said, *"do unto others before they do it to you."*

Yep. That was it. I'll never forget the wisdom in those words. Have you ever heard that? Great, so I'm not alone. And if that wasn't enough, he'd tag on this nugget: *"Don't forget the golden rule. He who has the gold makes the rules."*

When you really look at what was said, my Dad wasn't lying. But is that the best way to go through life? Sure, you might get by for a while and maybe even get over on a few people, but soon, your scheme gets busted. Back then, my Dad's words immediately began to shape my way of thinking. How much better for all that, at such an early and impressionable age when we're simply walking, talking little sponges that absorb everything, that our heads be filled with positive words and affirmation. If only my father would've said, *"Jesus is so good."*

Thanks to the path my Dad set before me, I began thinking of the kids at school who'd done me wrong or made fun of me. I started to devise schemes to pay them back one at a time. I should've been playing sandlot baseball and chatting with my pals about summer plans once school let out, but instead I'd become a devious schemer.

I recall my first effort into the world of living by my Dad's creed. I'd been planning my revenge for over a week while I stewed over what this kid had done to me. He had the nerve to make fun of the way I read out loud in class, and for that horrendous offense, he'd pay the price. Sneaking out of the cafeteria, I scurried back into our classroom and squeezed an entire bottle of Elmer's glue into his school bag. Sure, I destroyed everything in there his folks had bought for him, but that was what he deserved. According to my Dad, anyway. Oh, did I mention I was still in the first grade?

As I matured, so did my deviant retaliations. Another situation I recall taking great pride in was the great bicycle caper. Because I was the new kid at school, some boy thought it would be cool to kick my bike over in front of his friends. What he didn't know were two important things:

1. I was the new kid in a lot of schools because my Dad was a drunk and couldn't hold a job down, so we were always moving.
2. I was planning to sneak out of lunch period, steal his bicycle's safety chain's lock key, weave the plastic-coated anti-theft chain through the tire's spokes so he couldn't ride the bike and of course, throw the key away.

Guess what? It worked like a charm and instead of kicking my bike over again, he stood at the bike rack crying like a baby because he didn't know what to do. I'd never known so much satisfaction.

Unfortunately, what was actually occurring over those formative years was that my heart was being condition to stop feeling pain, empathy, regret or love. If you by chance are reading this book and it was you whom I did this to, please forgive me. I take no joy in the reality that this chapter could go on and on about the way I used to live my hurt-filled life.

While my Dad's perverse words were technically correct, they spiritually missed the mark. Sure the one who has the gold does make the rules, but what my Dad didn't realize was that it was God our Father who makes the rules because His streets are paved with gold. The rules of my Father do not condone revenge and petty, childish schemes to get other people before they get to you. No, God the Father forgives and loves us. Yes, even the kid who laughed at my reading and kicked over my bike. Most importantly, He even loves me, and He definitely loves you.

When we live a posture based on an eye for an eye, it causes us to always be on the lookout for another eye. Retaliation may feel good for the moment, but it drags us back to asking God why something bad always happened. You see, the flesh is never satisfied, and it always demands more. Our spirit will only sustain and fulfil us if it's from God.

I used to ask God all of the time why my life was so jacked up, because it felt like no matter how hard I tried something always came crashing into my plans. I thought God had forsaken me or was so disgusted with the way I turned out that He turned away from me. One day God caught me off guard when He answered my question with, "Try forgiving your father."

Yes, that's how God talks to me. There's not a lot of fancy King James Version literary prose. It's pretty straight forward. And for you dads who keep waiting on an answer from God…He is always answering. The problem is you might not be listening or willing to receive His answer. Too often we're looking for how to part the Red Sea and instead God is answering with "stop drinking so much, stop watching porn, stop doing drugs," and so on because all we need is Him. God will not bless you with much of anything until He can trust you to care for the little things.

When God told me to forgive my Dad, I knew it had to be Him because my Dad had already passed away. I know this chapter is supposed to be about forgiveness, but I wanted you to be with me to see, feel and maybe, just maybe, understand how easy unforgiveness can spread like a virus within us. I want you to know without a doubt that unforgiveness is a dark spirit from Satan, while forgiveness is a heart healing spirit from God.

We get asked all the time how we know that we truly forgave someone. This is the million-dollar question. God puts us at the right place at the right time. That question was posed to a friend of ours who was teaching on the power of forgiveness, and he said when it doesn't hurt anymore. I realized at that moment that when I forgave my Dad, even though he had passed many years prior, that the sting of his death didn't hurt anymore. I've had to forgive a lot of people in my life without actually talking with them and I've also had to ask for forgiveness from people I know I hurt without ever being able to speak with them, but the key is to forgive continually, and you will also be forgiven.

*"Let all bitterness and wrath and anger and clamor and slander be put away from you, along with malice. Be kind to one another, tenderhearted, forgiving one another, as God in Christ forgave you."*
Ephesians 4: 31-32

I realize now that I walked with unforgiveness in my heart and allowed it to permeate my life in a negative, destructive way. These personal things we're sharing with you are so that you will apply them in your own life. I'm sure you can see where you have allowed unforgiveness to steer you in a way you didn't want to go. Blessed are those who seek after Him and believe me, when I say it's never too late to forgive, I mean it is never too late to forgive.

I used to say they don't deserve my forgiveness, but then I'd flip the script and think what if Jesus said Richard doesn't deserve Me to forgive him. That is such a true statement because I don't deserve His mercy, but there is nothing I can do to stop it because it has already been given at the cross. God is always giving us a chance to forgive someone. I've learned that when I forgive the offender that the offense doesn't stick to me and it's much easier to let it go. Less baggage to carry through life, if you know what I mean.

Think of forgiveness as a muscle that tends to be weak and underdeveloped. At least for me it was. We want to challenge you to keep flexing your forgiveness muscle and in time it will get stronger. Strong enough to be a forgiveness trainer to someone else who is suffering in the prison in which most of us have been held captive. When we get paroled out of this cell it is true freedom. We can all walk tall without shame, without embarrassment and out from under condemnation.

Speaking from personal experience, unforgiveness causes distance between us and God. It will also cause distance between us and the family or people we love. We have to forgive, because holding on to grudges is like drinking poison and hoping the other person dies. What do you say we start to live before we die? Join me, join us and let's do this together. I love the men writing this book because they dare to be the hands and feet of Jesus, to share real feelings, emotions, hurts and victories with you, Dad.

# 7

# FATHERS WHO ARE PERFECTLY IMPERFECT

Wouldn't it be amazing to have it all figured out? We mean, how awesome to simply kick back and chill over the perfection of our dad, grandfather, great-grandfather, and so on. Meanwhile, we could brag about how flawless our kids are as those around applaud and take notes on how it's done. Maybe we're hosting conferences and work-shops on being the perfect dad who has never once messed up. What if they make a movie about us or, better yet, the world sends their kids to us be mentored in golden perfection.

And…snap out of it.

We all know that's a ridiculous notion. There is only one perfect Father and it's not any of us, but that doesn't give anyone license to stop trying. We are all coming from past experiences that could've been better. Our bet is your current parent-child relationship could use a little improvement too. And, for those fortunate men who had a pretty great dad growing up and are getting ready to glow with the haze of doing a bang-up job yourself, let's consider even the most remote possibility that there is room to grow.

Let's commit to taking off the mask hiding whatever it is that's hurting you. Is it an addiction, obsession, broken relationships, lost custody, behind on child support, struggling with another romantic relationship that's unhealthy for you and your child or maybe it's just general pain, agony or uncertain depression? Does this stuff affect the connection with your kid? Sure, it does, but it doesn't mean it has to control or define that relationship.

Everybody has messed up, but our past is not there to define us but to remind us of where we've been, so we'll know where we need to go. Drop the unrealistic fantasy and find peace. We are dads looking to improve and that makes us the perfect candidate for learning to become perfectly imperfect. Too often we beat ourselves up over past and present mistakes and assume our kids are judging us because of them. In an irrational response, we withdraw from them to either protect our ego or what we assume is our fatherly reputation. The hard truth is our kids need us. We want to give you a quick illustration about the dynamic with sons and dads no matter how bad you might've messed up in the past.

### Boys Need Dad

Boys love their mom, but they desperately need their dad. Prior to six years of age, boys are drawn to mom's nurturing gifts. Their physiology is still connected to the intimacy of pregnancy and birth, so it's all mom, all the time. But, when the little boy hits around six years old or so, they begin to identify with their dad's personality and style of play. They begin to solidify genetically encoded characteristics passed on through the generations. By the time puberty strikes and the boy's testosterone spikes 800%, he's actively seeking dad as his chaotic body is rushing full speed into manhood. The teenager needs his dad to guide him through these years.

Modeling is critical during this period. It's a form of monkey see, monkey do. No matter how imperfect we are, our kids are seeking us out. They are on a ballistic biological missile that cares less about your job trajectory and all about you personally being there. Statistically, this is a time when dads check out emotionally and physically. The usual causes for dads to focus elsewhere by this point have little to do with avoiding their child and more to do with focusing on their career, personal pursuits, divorce from their mom or an inability to manage their unmet expectations in life.

We covered the effects of boys and girls growing up in fatherless homes, but this example needed to be highlighted right here so you'd understand that while you're struggling with the pain, shame and guilt of what you feel are shackles of failure, your kid sees you as dad. We know everything we've done (good and not good) as well as all of our negative thoughts, disappointing decisions, missed opportunities and whatever else it is that makes us feel unworthy. The truth is you *are* unworthy. We all are, and that's where the grace and mercy of God the Father comes in. We are only made perfect through His redemption, not your latest promotion.

**How to Apply**

So, what does that mean to you in tangible terms as a dad? It means you're not perfect and no matter how many video games or trips to Disney World, you will always and only be you. The difference in broken you and renewed you is God. Kids in broken marriages that end in divorce do recover to engage in their own healthy relationships if they see a God-centered remarriage modeled. It's the same dynamic with dads. You can change and allow them to know when you changed and why you changed.

Telling kids that you changed for them isn't a good idea because it's usually based on a temporary emotion as opposed to a lasting decision centered on God. Also, the first time you disappoint them, and you will, there goes the well-meaning but unrealistic notion of newfound perfection. Instead, talk openly and honestly about your life, your struggles, hopes and dreams. Make sure you throw in there a few failures and what you've learned from them. Share your testimony with them along with your reliance on God as your model for becoming a better dad for them. In that model is the space for messing up, asking forgiveness, restoration and renewal. Above all, love abounds despite our past.

**Sharing Your Past**

Dad, this is big and while you may get second and sometimes third chances to reform the relationship with your kid, not coming straight today when asked can cost you huge in the future when discovered.

Talking about your past with your child sets the foundation for years to come. Handle it right, and they'll keep you in the loop. Mess it up and you might find yourself out in the cold, so we want to give you the information you'll need to do this right.

We want to reassure you that just because your kid gets curious and decides to ask you a question doesn't mean you crack like an egg and spill the beans. The key is finding balance between truth and age-appropriate sharing. Boundaries must always be maintained because long after that first conversation, you remain the father. You'll also have to determine if their questions are childish curiosity or quests for knowledge.

In your calculations for what and how much to share, keep in mind that if you want them to share with you, yet you refuse to shoot straight with them, then chances are they will always respond as you first responded to them. This is your time to set the standard. It's not like they are true crime detectives squeezing you for a confession. You are one of the most interesting, influential and hopefully accessible human beings in their life. Why wouldn't they be interested in knowing more about you? Some men are shocked at being asked questions by their kids. Don't be, because it's a sure sign of their investment into your life as their authority figure, mentor and dad.

The most common questions to expect are about what you were like as a kid, what kind of trouble did you get into and if you ever got spanked. Teens may ask about trying drugs, drinking alcohol or sex. As much as we profess we're going to speak openly with our kids about these topics, it's always tough to get going. So, when they initiate the talk, don't balk. Rehearse what you will and won't breach beforehand. Come across confident, honest and as always, loving.

We want to share a few tips that'll come in handy when talking to your kids.

**Remain On Target:**

It's required a lot of consideration, courage or chance taking for your kid to finally come to the point where they will open up and ask their dad a question about something other than what's on TV or where are we going for supper. Don't underestimate the importance of their initiated effort to know more about you. It's a key relationship building opportunity.

No matter what they ask you, do not refuse to answer, avoid their question or switch subjects. You may never get a second chance, so be prepared. Remember, they are kids and their skill at presenting questions aren't as highly honed as an investigative reporter. Give them grace and even help reform their inquiry if needed to make sure you give them exactly what information they are seeking.

But don't water down or reconfigure their intent as your way of getting out of telling the truth. Say for example they ask about drug use and you snap back that they should not ask about that, then what they now know is they cannot and will not ever come to you if they have a question or issue involving drugs.

They also realize that they can't talk to you about serious topics in their own life. Your defensive response also signals that there are taboo topics in the family, and of course because you refused to answer, they now think you were and possibly still are a major drug user or head of some cartel. And the biggest problem your refusal has caused is that your child realizes if you won't share with them, then they won't share with you. Remember what we said about modelling, or monkey see, monkey do?

Your first opportunity to shine like a superstar dad is lost, and now you and they both fall into a vast chasm that will widen over time. They will not pull themselves up by their bootstraps, charge back in there and ask you again. Instead, they skulk off with their wounded spirit and stop asking you anything. Soon, they won't even talk to you because they've found answers from peers who are confused as they are, adults who have sinister motives for befriending your child or the internet where nothing but porn and propaganda wait to suck them into their destructive web.

Even if you've already experienced this episode and handled it imperfectly, you are still dad. God the Father modelled redemption, and you have the potential for redeeming yourself by restoring the relationship. You dropped the ball, so you have to pick it up. If you have to apologize for balking, then they will see you in your humility and humanity. Even if you have to remind them of the incident, let them know you messed up and you want to correct your mistake. Giving them the respect of asking for a second chance allows you and them to both experience the Fatherly model of confession, forgiveness, restoration and renewal. Bridges can be rebuilt, but you're the one swinging the hammer. Make sure you hit the mark!

**Honesty is Non-Negotiable:**

Kids may not have a clue about what's going on around them other than friends and video games, but when it comes to a parent feeding them a line of bull, they detect it quicker than they smell supper from upstairs. Do not, and we repeat, do not ever lie to them when they ask about your past. Most of our fears in telling them details about what we did in our youth are rooted in an expectation that they will then head out of the house to do the exact same things.

Explain to them that the person who did those things is not the same person who is now an adult and their parent. Maybe sharing how your own parents' influence or lack of engagement in your life as a child created chaos and dangerous opportunities for placing yourself out into jeopardizing behaviors that you regret.

Sharing the truth about past indiscretions does not signal permission or implied consent for them to repeat that behavior. Truth telling, even when it's painful shows them the value and importance of also telling the truth. It may seem insignificant at the time, but it's planting a seed in your relationship that will blossom in the future because they will respect you for telling them the truth.

Remember, they are usually at a last-ditch effort before working up the courage to ask you something sensitive. Give them the respect for making the effort and also understand that by turning them away, you may just be turning then out alone or into the presence of someone with ill intentions.

**Communications Are Key:**

"Later," is a destructive response to give your child when they've made an effort to talk with you. You might've had the worst day ever, or they might be acting like a royal spoiled brat, but don't allow emotions or what you consider as bad behavior to become an excuse to excuse yourself from dealing directly with your child.

While we understand you may be thinking this all sounds like the child gets to dictate the times and terms of the conversations, the truth is, the most opportune times to engage in trust building is when they are open and receptive to it. Once they know you are sincerely an open door, they'll reciprocate the effort to pay attention when you start the conversation. Their desire to talk with you is based not only on you being dad, but also that you were once their age and faced the same temptations that they now face in the way of school, friends, drugs, drinking, sex and the many other issues they have to deal with.

Your willingness and actually honoring the offer to be an open door gives your child the security they need to know that even if they don't want to talk about it with you, you are indeed there when and if they do. They are looking for your wisdom no matter how you may have messed up in your past and even the not-so-distant past. Being imperfectly perfect allows you to teach from experience while offering valuable lessons learned.

Commit to never judging them for what they are asking or sharing with you. We realize it's easier said than done, but they're also looking for the way you respond as much as what you say. By communicating openly and often and always in love, you help them establish their sense of self-esteem. They will learn to face tough times and hard conversations with you and others by the way you model truth telling with them.

**Perfectly Imperfect Conversations:**

Who wants to talk with a know-it-all anyways? Your child sees you for who you are, their dad. You are amazing at times and not so amazing at others. If you don't think your child sees that in you then you are fooling yourself. They may not know what demons you're fighting or details from your past that still haunt you today, but they see the cracks in your armor. How else could they so masterfully get under your skin?

Get comfortable with the act of talking with your child while establishing appropriate boundaries and common sense. You can and should always answer their questions but ground the information you share in sharing what adds value to their inquiry. Droning on about something you experienced that falls outside of the boundaries of age and maturity appropriateness only causes them confusion and risks your losing credibility.

If you're addressing a situation that was resolved in your past, then share what actions you took to overcome them. There might actually be something you're still dealing with that can shed light on the tensions caused between you and your child. Kids don't fully comprehend the depths of guilt, pain and shame as it effects their lives, but your perseverance in overcoming a current situation might be helpful to them as an example of actively handling the situation head on.

Kids are just like adults when it comes to being drawn to an honest account of flawed people and their efforts to overcome. Everyone loves an underdog story even if that underdog is their dad. The trials along your journey aren't just old memories you might rather forget; they may serve a higher purpose in teaching your child that your decisions have had consequences and so will theirs.

It takes an active balancing effort to share without oversharing. You should think through the possibilities of being questioned one day. If you were divorced, arrested, fought addiction or something that has left a trail, then you can be assured your child will discover it. Especially in this era of social media and public records access, don't get caught off guard when confronted by an informed question.

Being prepared establishes your position as an authority in their life as well as allowing them to see that no matter what you might have done before, you are present now and love them enough to share with them.

---

### Juan's Session:

Out of everything my fellow dads shared so far, I love what George said in his section of this chapter. That fits me perfectly because I am the perfectly imperfect father and I'm okay with that. We each have lots of chances to work at making needed changes in our lives so that we can connect better with our kids. I understand that my performance is imperfect, and I'll make many mistakes, but my position being centered on God the Father is total perfection.

The Bible says in Ephesians 1, *"Blessed is the God and Father of our Lord Jesus Christ, who has blessed us with every spiritual blessing in the heavens in Christ."* Wow, guess what? I think Ephesians 1 mentions "in Christ" about fifteen times because it's critical that we as dads understand our position must be rooted in Christ. Once we align ourselves as sons of God the Father, then we will know His grace as dads even when we do mess up. And we will.

When my imperfect position is aligned next to the perfection of God, I enjoy an intimate relationship with the Holy Spirit and get to experience love, joy, peace, patience, kindness, goodness, faithfulness and self-control. And because we only know what we know, once we know these fruits of the Spirit, we can then show them to our own kids. We want to become better dads, so learning from the ultimate Father is the only way to be the better dad. The better we know our heavenly Father, the more we act like our heavenly Father.

I've messed up many times by getting angry with my children and even yelling at my son when he fell to addiction, but once I'd been shown God's grace, I was able to also show that same love and grace to them. God opened that better dad door for me once I learned that humility helps me to ask for help while pride says I can do it by myself. James 4:6 (TPT) says, *"But he continues to pour out more and more grace upon us. For it says, God resists you when you are proud but continually pours out grace when you are humble."*

Pride blocks the ability to receive God's grace and because we are imperfect, we really have to understand that it's only by grace that we'll remain teachable. If we remain humble and teachable, then we are ripe for growing into the perfect dads that reflect our Lord and Savior. Take a look at Proverbs 4 (TPT):

*"Listen to my correction, my sons, for I speak to you as your father. Let discernment enter your heart and you will grow wise with the understanding I impart. ² My revelation-truth is a gift to you, so remain faithful to my instruction.³ For I, too, was once the delight of my father and cherished by my mother—their beloved[ child." ⁴ Then my father taught me, saying, "Never forget my words. If you do everything that I teach you, you will reign in life."*

*5 So make wisdom your quest—search for the revelation of life's meaning.*
*Don't let what I say go in one ear and out the other.*

My advice to you is as long as you are open to following God's instruction, you will continue to grow into the amazing dad God created you to be.

### Scott's Session:

"Tell us the one about when you were drunk in the back of the truck and threw all of the money out onto the highway." I looked into all of the bright eyes staring at me from around our dining room table and knew I'd said way too much. Yeah, I was less than perfect in my youth and on occasion I'd failed to consider my audience when recounting occasions from my misspent past.

Stopping to reflect, I hadn't realized it, but almost every story I shared with my kids about my childhood through college years involved violence, alcohol or rebellious behavior. It was a dysfunctional childhood, and I'd handled it horribly where explaining it to my kids was involved. I always hid the pain of those years by making light of it, but to a pack of sponges who soaked up every word and forgot absolutely nothing, I'd screwed up in my initial approach.

Sure, I was imperfect, but instead of sharing exploits that ignited their immature imaginations without explaining the consequences of my actions, I was careless. It was that question from our oldest daughter who was in her senior year of high school that landed the knockout punch to my better senses. They were all well-behaved kids and Leah and I never hesitated to share our expectations for them. That included warning them against drinking, drugs and risky behavior. Yet, I'd shared more than a few old stories that glamorized the very behavior we forbad.

Being a dad is not something perfect men do. Actually, it's the opportunity to learn from our mistakes and help point others to the one perfect Father. That's exactly what I did in the silent gap between being asked that question about throwing cash and giving an account of my actions. I asked God to forgive me for being so reckless and how to fix it. God the Father was so kind and gave me the perfect answer. He said point them to Him.

"Guys," I cleared my throat. "I'm sorry for making that night seem like a lot of fun." They waited patiently for the punch line, but there was none. I continued with the rest of the story. "That money I threw out of the back of a truck was everything my business had made for the week. It was meant for paying bills and employees. I was reckless and it caused a lot of people to suffer. I'm so ashamed of what I did and thanks to the merciful God, my life was spared. It's only thanks to Him that I am here today."

I know the truth of hearing me confess my wicked ways and professing God's grace caught their attention. It sure caught mine. My imperfect past is important for our kids to be aware of because in sharing they see that they aren't alone in their errors. They also see that I'm always honest and open with them even about things that don't shine the best light on me. But those are always my chances to instead shine the light of God the Father. Our kids can know we aren't perfect while more importantly knowing we are forgiven and redeemed by a God who is.

**Richard's Session:**

I think this one chapter could be a great title for a life changing book. This chapter could truly be the beginning of many books or the deeper insight of many dads. I know this now because most us were taught to believe the lie that was spoken over us before we were ever taught the truth.

*Trust in the Lord with all your heart and lean not into your own understanding.*
Proverbs 3:5

Well you have read enough about me to know what I was taught and to see the misdirection I traveled. Most of all I want you to know that it didn't just happen all at one time. It was an accumulation of hurts, mistrust and disappointments sandwiched in between doubt, self-worth and lack of confidence. That's the perfect recipe for true-life dump cake.

Before you even finish this book, it's important to make the choice for giving your life to Christ. If you haven't, now is the perfect time. If you already have, then now is the time to rededicate your commitment to God the Father. Don't miss this opportunity because you've told yourself that you're too far gone and have caused too much pain and there's too much bad water under the bridge. These are some of the lies we were told and still believe without question.

If I told you that you could still change, you can still make wrong things right, you would think about it and probably doubt me. I've lived that life and I am still standing to promise you that the lies you were taught are simply that—lies. Dad, you do have what it takes. You were created in the image of God. Through the Holy Spirit you are equipped with love, joy, peace, patience, kindness, faithfulness, gentleness and self-control. Even though we are all born with God-given potential for these beautiful gifts, they still have to be activated through a life lived for God the gift giver.

God let me go and grow through the most difficult of valleys so that He and He alone could get the praise for it. If these things just came naturally to us, it would mean we could lean on our own understanding because we would be so proud we wouldn't need God. He gives us many opportunities to learn each of these gifts because they will make our lives better, not easier. Life it hard and most of the time unfair, but we serve a true, fair Father.

We have to remember that what we do on earth is temporary and must switch from an earthly mindset to a kingdom mindset. So dads, the next time you're ready to light into junior over what he's done wrong (#overcorrecting), take the time to show them everything they're doing right. Balancing correction and celebration is the key.

God focuses on relationships instead of rules. Rules are what most religions try to shove down your throat and quickly run people off. Loving people is what God does and He wants you to focus more on the relationship with your kid than always harping on the rules. Once we come into that loving relationship with the Father, we learn how to mirror that same relationship with our child.

That most important relationship with God the Father must be in place before we can move forward with anyone else. The best and only way to build that incredible relationship is by communicating with God through prayer.

*16 Rejoice always, 17 pray without ceasing, 18 give thanks in all circumstances; for this is the will of God in Christ Jesus for you.*
1 Thessalonians 5:16-18

In my beginning faith walk I couldn't wrap my head around the idea of praying without stopping. I thought, how can you do anything if you are just constantly praying? But in time and in the process of living out my Christian walk I began to give thanks all of the time. I am always praying about my life, my choices, my short comings. You too will see that it becomes second nature.

Everything on the pages of this book comes with time as long as we are seeking the kingdom of God. When are we as dads going to get tired of doing it wrong, suck it up and try a way that is going to work for once? Lord knows we've tried everything under the sun to no avail. Please know that none of us are perfect and have all the answers but we know who does. We have fumbled, dropped the ball, and have thrown many interceptions. We have missed the tackles of life, missed easy field goals and have drawn many penalties, but our head coach doesn't count any of that against us. As a matter of fact, He forgets these stats. He only counts how many times we get back into the game.

Look on the bright side like I do, there are many writers better than me, more handsome, smarter, richer, more qualified, taller, faster...you get the picture. If I focused on someone else's gifting, I would never become the dad God has called me to be. You know I like to look at it like this: there's always an original that changes the world and often people want to imitate the greatness. Take Elvis for example. There are men who still do impersonations of him because he was so good, but they can never take the place of the real deal. You are the real deal. Elvis has already been done but guess what? You and I have not. So let your gift shine.

You have something so incredible in you that the enemy of your soul pursues you nonstop to steal it from you because he doesn't have it and never will. Stop cowering down and rise up. Get back in the game because it is a lot more fun than the splinters on the sideline bleachers.

When you catch that proverbial one-handed touchdown and you do your very own original version of the Ickey Shuffle, give praise with a huge smile and point to the heavens because God was the one who paved the way to the end zone.

### George's Session:

Out of all the chapters in this book I think this is the chapter that fits me perfectly! I am perfectly imperfect as a father, but I am okay with that as we've all got a lot of work that needs to be done in our lives. When I was a young man there was a song that had a verse that said, "Please be patient with me, God's not through with me yet." That seems to be a good life verse for me.

In the last chapter on fathers that forgive, I shared with you a few instances that showed my glaring imperfections as a son. In many ways I had forgotten about some of my youthful mistakes until inquiring minds just had to know. Over the years as my kids grew up, they became inquisitive about my life as a teenager and how I over-came common temptations that all kids face at some point in their adolescent years. In fact, my daughter Camryn made it a habit when-ever we rode in the car together for me to tell her a new story so she could get to know me better. Inevitably some of my stories showed her and my son just how perfectly imperfect their father was as a son.

Generally retelling the stories was a fun and exciting trip down memory lane. But there were times when the kids had their mouths wide open in shock at my choices and immature behavior. A lot of the shock came as a result of my kids coming to a realization that their dear old dad was not a choir boy (although I actually did sing in the church choir). He had been around the block and experienced a few things that I should not have experienced and that many times were hurtful to me and my parents. There have even been a few tense moments when parenting that my kids have reminded me that I did some of the very things I was asking them not to participate in as teenagers.

It was in those moments that I had to really humble myself. I had to admit that I had done lots of things wrong and out of order in the way God had designed and that my parents required. Trust me, no dad, let alone a pastor, wants his kids justifying wrongdoing because of his example. So I found myself being transparent about my wrongdoings yet trying to let my own kids realize some of the hurt and pain that my choices had caused in my life and others. What I was saying as a parent was not that I was perfect. Just the opposite; I am perfectly imperfect. What I was asking was to learn from my mistakes and hard-headed misfortunes.

My Dad always taught me that God never wastes a hurt or an experience. He taught me that God is a redeemer and could use our hurts and his deliverance as lessons for the next generation. Hopefully my kids and your kids can learn from our mistakes and missed opportunities to get it right the first time. As dads and men, we are pictures of God's grace and our stories are a part of his redemptive nature in our lives. We cannot afford to not tell our kids our sins of the past and how we missed the mark.

In John 5, Jesus comes across a sick man at a pool. The man had been sick for 38 years with no one to help him. Jesus eventually heals the man but says something that has always stuck with me. Jesus said, "Get up, pick up your mat, and walk" (John 5:8). The mat represented his bed of affliction and pain. But why would Jesus tell the man after he is healed to take his mat with him when he would no longer need his sick bed? Surely, he would have no need for his sick bed of pain and affliction since he was healed. Then it dawned on me, the mat was not for him but for all the people who knew the man had been healed after being sick for 38 years. It was his redemption story not to hide and forget but to show all that only God can deliver from such a morbid past. Men it's okay to tell your children you are perfectly imperfect. Even more, you are a picture of God's grace and redemption.

# 8

# FATHERS WHO LOVE BEYOND BIOLOGY

"You're not my real dad," Jesus said.

Okay, maybe we're putting words in the mouth of a 12-year-old Jesus when His mom and dad asked where He'd been after they had been separated from Him for three days. And although His parents must have known Jesus wasn't the typical preteen boy, they were indeed His parents, and rightfully concerned about Him. Yes, even Joseph, His stepfather.

As men, fathers or stepfathers, we can relate to Joseph in this moment. It had to sting a little when Jesus replied, *"Why were you looking for me? Did you not know that I must be in my Father's house?"* (Luke 2:49).

Consider this for a moment—Jesus, the Lord and Savior of the world, was raised by Joseph, His stepfather. We never really thought about it in that context until we began talking about the challenges of blended families. It's completely possible but takes hard, consistent work to successfully mix families. Men are often without a foundation for establishing their authority where their wife's children are concerned. This is one of the most common causes of divorce among spouses who attempted to enter into a blended scenario.

• • •

Where do dads (stepdads) go for direction in preparing for their new role? To the one perfect Father of course. But how is the role of being a stepfather addressed in the Bible? Just what authority do stepfathers have in the lives of a blended family's children? Let's ask WWJD —What Would Joseph Do?

Even when spouses agree to share complete responsibility of parenting to include discipline and mentoring, the difference between theory and reality often has both spouses at odds with each other. The truth is, it takes a daily rhythm to give authority to the non-biological parent for your kids and receive permissible authority from your spouse for your non-biological kids. This cautious balancing act doesn't take much to go off of the rails. We dads are leaders, doers and fixers by nature. When we feel as if something is inaccessible, we tend to rebel against it.

Guys don't handle emotional assaults or ego jabs very well. Even the smallest slight can come across like a major attack on our manhood... especially coming from a child. Many blended relationships fail because the man of the house can't, or won't, invest the time and effort to mesh with the children.

"I'm not going to be talked to like that by a child."

Have you said that, or maybe it's sizzling at the tip of your tongue and only held in check by a maximum effort of restraint? If you've not said it, then you're one of the rare few who haven't. This is a judgement free zone, but that declarative statement is one of the most common battle cries quoted by moms to either counselors or divorce attorneys.

We've also heard men say it, because in fact, it is an all too popular last straw before we retreat and eventually surrender. Passivity is the sin that men resort to when we've been emotionally wounded through what we perceive as disrespect. If we can't be in charge of it, then we're throwing our hands in the air and forgetting about it. That's apathetic passivity and it's one hundred and eighty degrees against the grain of who God ordained us to be.

Of course, the other side of the coin is the sin behavior of a woman's defiant independence. We're talking about marriage covenant independence as in acting separate, apart and often in contrast to her husband. When the mother elevates her kids above her husband (their stepfa-

ther), that's not only against the supernatural order of the home's hierarchy, but it's a rebellious act of contrary behavior. Moms often behave
this way when they feel insecure, and it's illustrated by her natural
defense of her child. And just like that, the battle lines have been
drawn. There are few things in life that polarize positions than a
mom's defense of her children and a man's response to feeling disre-
spected.

If you're wondering why this scenario is such an emotional flash point,
it's because of the respective languages men and women speak. Men,
as you know, speak the language of respect. Women speak the
language of security. You are the spiritual head of your household and
that position inherently seeks to be respected by all who reside or visit.
Having to bear the brunt of a non-biological child's disdain is an easy
tripwire to stumble across. But, as that spiritual head of the home,
there's much more to it than sitting at the head of the dining room
table and barking orders. Our anointing requires us to model God the
Father in showing grace and love to all who enter. Yep, that also means
her kids who tap dance on glass across your last nerve.

There is a better way than fueling the cycle of you feeling hurt, aggressively saying something about the kids, then your wife coming to their
protection and engaging with them without you and so on and so on
and so on. It's your time to shine as the leader, and what better way to
lead than by a biblical example of a stepfather that can only come
through God's Word.

**The Joseph Example**

When it comes to kids, being a commanding, manly man at domestic
war doesn't cut it. Learning to stepparent as a godly man among your
blended family is the answer. The interaction we mentioned earlier
between a young Jesus and His parents says plenty about Joseph and
his character as a stepfather. Like many men, Joseph could've easily
snapped back by asserting his earthly authority as an adult. Instead, he
understood and encouraged the relationship Jesus sought with His real
Father. It didn't diminish Joseph's role; it strengthened it.

Let's take a quick look at the interaction described in Luke. It all began
in the proper tone when Mary took a unified stance with her husband:

*"Your father and I have been searching for you in great distress."* (Luke 2:48).

When spouses don't communicate, one spouse can alienate the other when dealing with an issue concerning the children. Mary, in this case, didn't alienate Joseph. She made sure Jesus knew they were both worried and were out looking for Him. It's important for the kids to know that you both love them. Don't assume they know how you feel. Not saying or showing it because you're the strong, silent type is only interpreted by kids that you don't care about them.

Of course, even though Jesus understood who His true Father was, He respected Joseph's authority as an earthly dad: *"And he went down with them and came to Nazareth and was submissive to them."* (Luke 2:51). It's probably safe to assume that Joseph earned that reverence through a lifetime of pursuing a loving relationship with his stepson, Jesus.

Allow this illustration to encourage you that no matter how awesome or absent the kids' connection with their biological dad may be, there is endless capacity for a loving relationship with you.

**Being Dad**

Without blending your family on biblical principles, each spouse will become more territorial on their side of the line in the sand. Gradually, neither will be willing or able to meet in the middle and come to a compromise. Here are a few ways you can be the kind of dad that Joseph was.

First, for those who are dating, accept her and her kids. Her kids are not your competition. If you get married, they will be your responsibility. Believe it or not, you and her kids are vying for the same things from her—love, time and attention. Her kids have already been through enough. Either add value to the family unit, or don't ask her to marry you.

Second, if you're already married and have hard feelings toward the kids, pray for God to change your heart. They need a Christian male role model, not a job-site foreman. No matter their ages, they are your beloved wife's children. Give them that respect. You are the adult—always hold yourself in that humble esteem.

Third, you are not in competition with their biological dad. Encourage a healthy relationship with him. They will respect you for that.

One last guideline that we've used: Always consider the way you as a child would want to be treated or how you want your own child treated. Then do that. It all goes back to Jesus's golden rule. *"So whatever you wish that others would do to you, do also to them..."* (Matthew 7:12).

Be proud of the opportunity and the gift given to you. You were never forced to be a dad to her kids, and because you choose to marry their mom you also chose to parent them. That makes you special because you made the decision as a leader, mentor and nurturer to love them as a dad. Loving beyond biology is something to be proud of, Dad. We respect you for making that choice.

---

### Scott's Session:

When Leah and I began dating, we talked often about our kids and the challenges of blending families. We understood how difficult it could be and the data surrounding the high rates of failure and divorce. Determined not to become a negative statistic, we'd do everything in our power to ensure this merger wouldn't fail.

Leah had four very young ones and I had Max. Chronologically he fell in between hers. Max also has Down syndrome and although it had always been just him with me at home, I assumed he'd love the four new kids in his life. Isn't theory versus reality another funny thing? The truth is that all because Leah and I loved each other and couldn't wait to do life together didn't mean our kids shared that same level of enthusiasm.

Kids, cash, and sex are the top three causes of divorce, and when the family is blended, it adds extra tension. Still, we were determined to face it all head on and not only survive but thrive. Honestly, I was struggling. Overprotective of Max was an understatement. When I saw one of Leah's kids not catering to Max the way I used to, I'd quickly set them straight. Of course, her kids have always been above and beyond in their relationship with Max. Also, Max may have special needs, but the boy is all boy and tough as a cobb. He's given the kids many more bumps and bruises than he's received in their natural roughhousing.

Still, it was a challenge for me to be completely open with Leah's crew. I wasn't sure what to say or how to act. All I knew was what it was like to command people in my career. Soon, I resorted to giving orders and shaping up my own tiny tikes special operations group. They didn't need extra discipline. They needed love. Yet, because my Dad had never shown love, I defaulted to what I knew, which was giving orders.

God the perfect Father soon led me into a relationship with Larry Titus. He would immediately become my spiritual father and serve as a real-life example of how a man was ordained to show unconditional love to their children. Yes, even if the kids weren't biologically his. Dad was always quick to remind me that all he was doing was showing the Father's love.

I'd never had that Christlike relationship with my own Dad, and because it was causing me to stumble in the connection with Leah's kids, God graciously gifted me with the blessing of my non-biological spiritual father. Dad actually showed me in very tangible examples of how we were adopted into God's kingdom with full rights, access and authority in the same way I was adopted into Dad's family. This concrete example allowed me to clearly understand that it's not about biology, but it's love that makes a father. Of course, once I mirrored the way Dad loved me, I in turn began showing love to Leah's kids in that same manner. I also knew that I wasn't loving our kids like Dad, but like God the Father. That love is uninhibited, endless and beyond biology.

### Richard's Session:

"Do as I say not as I do," is often used by broken parents who, although they think what they're doing is right, are actually still strug-gling to keep their own lives strung together. I've heard it and said it more times than I care to confess. Sheri and I have been fortunate enough to sit with hundreds, if not thousands of couples to help coach and understand the issues within their personal faith walk and marriages. It's no secret that we all seem to have issues with raising and disciplining our kids. Did you catch that last word? Disciplining. Isn't it very close to the word discipling?

I'm going to share as a father in a blended family who had custody of my biological 5- and 7-year-old children. My wife's daughter had just moved out to attend college. Right now, I love my kids dearly, but back then I'm not so sure I knew what love meant. Love means you're willing to change hurtful behaviors at your expense to increase the security of the people around you. This mainly applies to your family in respect to building them up emotionally.

My first step was having the heart to make whatever changes were required and God did the rest. But before I came to that understanding, my marriage was horribly broken and I gave it a lame attempt to have the Norman Rockwell family. Actually, we were more like the Simpsons but probably even more like the Lannisters from *Game of Thrones*.

When I was dating Sheri, she told me she was going to write a book about raising children, and after I met her daughter Tara, I was sure she could do it. But two months after living together and Sheri being with my kids, all aspirations of writing a book were out the window. You see, by raising my children—that's right, at this point in our relationship my kids were only my kids. No one was going to tell me how to raise my kids because I would not allow Sheri to step on my parental toes.

I hope you can see the disfunction and separation that was starting right there. It was just a spark before the big explosion. She was seeing a need for discipline, love, direction, accountability and the list goes on. I was seeing children hurt by divorce. So I took a lackadaisical approach. I thought they had been hurt too much already, so I didn't want to be too strict with them. You're seeing this right? I was creating the monster that was to come. Not intentionally, of course.

*My people will be destroyed for their lack of knowledge.*
Hosea 4:6

Whenever Dylan or Hannah would get in trouble we would take their phones or video games away. By the way, if I could do it over again they would have had phones that only called or texted us, no data! Hear me parents, the video games would not have been violent. Trying to punish or discipline a child by taking away a violent game only brought out a violent reaction from the child, and we sit and wonder where that came from.

Phones with pictures, that's all I'm saying read between the lines. Also Sheri and I would say. "You are grounded for a week child," only to have me reinstate whatever was the leverage back within a couple of days because once again they have suffered too much already. Life has suffering and there I was playing God again, trying to minimize the hurt. Sometimes God is trying to use that hurt to draw us closer to Him so He can teach us He is the healer of hurts. Because of me changing the game rules all the time my wife and I started to argue more, then the arguing grew to resentment, then the resentment grew to isolation. All this was happening because we lost whatever unity we had just by not being in complete agreement with anything.

*Finally, brothers, rejoice. Aim for restoration, comfort one another, agree with one another, live in peace; and the God of love and peace will be with you.*
2 Corinthians 13:11

We struggled because we are both type A driven personalities. As we met with couples, we saw some of the same similarities. The husband trying to over-discipline her kids because he is the man of the house. He's determined not to put up with their bad behavior but remember that rules without relationship equals rebellion 100% of the time. Now, in the husband's defense he just wanted her children to love him. You have to understand that every blended family is completely different, very different dynamics, but we all want the same thing. Children who are healthy and balanced right? Well, parents who are not healthy and balanced will not have children who are healthy and balanced for the most part. Funny how we keep mentioning this over and over. But God will get things in order.

*"Trust in the Lord with all your heart, and lean not on your own understanding. In all your ways acknowledge Him, and He will make your paths straight".*
Proverbs 3:5-6

I wish somebody had told us in the beginning that since there was no relationship with each other's children, the biological parent needs to be the heavy with their biological children to help usher in a relationship with the stepparent. I hate the word step; who created that word? A step is something you place under your foot. We prefer the word Bonus. Bonus mom and bonus dad means an added reward for good behavior. We have to look at the best in people even though we have been groomed to look for the negative.

Remember when I said in earlier chapters, we were taught the wrong before we were taught the right? We must be willing to have a teachable spirit, so when our spouse talks to us even in a tone that's hard to receive, we can still listen and defuse explosive situations. Wives can have a tendency to be controlling but we as husbands need to know where this originates from. It's because they have had to do our job most of their lives not even aware they are doing it. As passive males, we don't like confrontation, so we tend to just let things happen. Instead of letting the family fall apart, wives step in and try to run everything and hold it all together. As men, we see it as nagging and we have to ask why are they nagging? Usually it's because we are out of the position we were created to be in, and they are in a position they were never created to hold. She is our helpmate; she was created by God the Father to see things we cannot see. I have learned the hard way to seek her thoughts, feelings and discernment about everything, because it always seems to work out for our best.

I always think of the scripture that one can put to flight 1000 but two can put to flight 10,000 because the Lord is with them. Men let's lay our pride down, let's bring our wives into the fold, let's love our children and her children by taking them out and spending quality time. It's all about our relationship with our spouse, our children, our family, and our God. Without a true and healthy relationship with God, we cannot have a healthy relationship with anyone else.

### George's Session:

It's rare to hear these days, but my parents were married for over half a century (fifty-two years) before my father passed away. He would often say proudly that he was the husband to only one wife. For him it was a badge of honor. I grew up wanting to wear that same badge of honor and for a quarter of a century now I have been the husband to one wife. By the grace of God I have not personally experienced the nuances of being a part of a blended family. I do, however, understand that it is very common in today's society and many families have found the answers to making it work.

Despite personally not having a blended family and navigating the intricacies of parenting stepchildren in my home, for years I have taken to heart the challenge of loving beyond biology. Especially in view of what I think is an epidemic of fatherlessness that continues to impact our contemporary society. Growing up in the south it was common for men and other fathers to help guide and mentor young men in the community. It was common to hear the African proverb "it takes a village to raise a child." Helping to care for others is a part of my DNA.

As a pastor for over twenty-five years one of the joys of my life has been to help parent spiritual sons and daughters who have come faith in Christ within my ministry context. In the church world we called this process discipleship. Whether it's been as a mentor, teacher, marriage or life coach, I've had to lovingly and graciously father many on their personal journey. You don't have to have biological kids to make a difference in the lives of other kids or young adults. You simply have to be willing to invest the time it takes to make a deposit in the next generation.

My father taught me a profound principle—time equals love. There is so much wisdom in that simple statement. What it really suggests is if you love people, especially the next generation, there must be a will-ingness to help father the fatherless. In order to make a difference in the lives of others it often takes an investment of time and patience. I can hear my Dad now saying, "Son, people don't care how much you know until they know how much you care." Caring takes time.

As an NFL Chaplain for the Los Angeles Chargers, I have the privilege of mentoring and coaching young men who have made it to the elite level of pro sports. They are some of the most focused and committed young men I know. Each rookie class that enters the locker room for the first time comes with many young men who are in relative prox-imity to my son's age and maturity in life. Sure, they make lots of money, but they are in need of the same simple wisdom, instruction and direction that I share with my own son. Whether it's advice on relationships or issues with character development, they all need direction at some point.

So whether you are a biological dad, stepdad or father to the fatherless, it's all the same. You never graduate from being a father and mentor to someone either in your home, at work or perhaps just down the street. So when the going gets tough and you think you are not up for the challenge, I want to leave you with this piece of advice from a sign I once read: you were made for this!

### Juan's Session:

Loving beyond biology is a beautiful thing. It's an action that began with a choice. You were given the power to make that choice to love someone as a father. It's the same way God the Father chooses to love us, and it touches my heart. I often find myself in tears as emotions surface while I'm praying, writing or just hanging out. I love my family so dearly because God first loved me.

Of course it wasn't always that way, you know. Tears fall at the futile wish of turning back the hands of time. It's not uncommon for me to grab the phone and start texting my kids to tell them they're special. I want them to know that my heart is broken about not being there earlier in their lives. I want them to never have a single doubt that I love them dearly. But the truth is, we men do get distracted by the busyness of life and time slips right by.

We've got to be intentional by first spending time with God so He'll plant that seed of desire in our preoccupied hearts to stop what we're doing and share time with our kids. We need our Father's love and attention just as our kids need us and God the Father. Our position in Christ aligns all relationships no matter if they are with our biological kids, our step kids or even people with no connection to our family. Loving beyond biology doesn't stop beyond the family tree.

Also beyond biology is age. It doesn't matter how old they are, our kids need our love. Our kids range from teens to thirties. Because I'd walked away from my own kids early on and then didn't meet Ruthy's kids until we blended our families, we all got a late start growing family roots. Let me encourage you to start right now in building the bonds of a strong connection with your kids no matter their DNA relationship.

I'm pretty chill now that I'm living for Jesus, but truth be told, being a stepdad and blending families isn't the easiest thing I've done. It can also push you to your limits. What has served our family well and is important for you to do is to communicate. It can be a tough challenge but don't stop talking. Most of the conversations were focused on creating priorities, boundaries and roles for everyone in the family.

No matter what our individual stories were, when we all came together it was possible only because of first being reconciled through God the Father. We call ourselves the Hispanic Brady Bunch, and it's possible thanks to God the Father. The Bible says we all have the ministry of reconciliation, so when we have Christ in our lives, not only are we reconciled back to God the Father, but through the cross, we remain united.

Yep, I get worked up over family because it is God's gift to us. I love to write about my family, talk about my family and share the miraculous testimony of my family. We were absolutely broken into dust until God picked us up, restored us and allowed us to come together in His love. Speaking of talking about family, I just got off with the phone with Scott. I was so emotional that again tears poured down my face, but I wasn't embarrassed talking to my brother and co-author. We're all that in love with our kids and being a dad.

While talking about blended families, I told Scott that we were adopted into God's family. He said God chose to love us even though He wasn't obligated to do so. What a beautiful picture of God's grace. Isn't that amazing? I believe everything has to do with God's kingdom agenda. So your family, even your blended family has a purpose, and as parents it's our responsibility to develop and train them in the ways of the Lord. That includes loving beyond biology.

# 9

# FATHERS WHO GROW

The most accurate statement a dad might hear over the years is that he's changed or that he's not the same dad he once was. Of course, we're assuming those comments were offered as a reflection of positive change and improvement, but the truth is, change occurs along your trajectory in life and certainly as dad. The potential for a dad to be the same person he was when his child was born as opposed to now as the dad to a teenager or adult would be virtually impossible.

The natural life cycle suggests and requires imminent change. At the most chronological core you are going to age as you move through life. Although some of us wish we could stop the clock or fight against it, time does indeed march on. That's one of the inevitable trajectories of life. Along that time continuum are the elements of wisdom, maturity, perspective and experience among other variables that help shape who we are. Since being a dad is a component attached to the life trajectory, it's only natural to expect change. Therefore, it's a fact that the dad we were when our child was born is not the same dad we are at whatever age your child is today.

Growing as dad includes a progression in the relationship we share with our child. We say progress because that would include the healthy changes in a parent-child relationship. Becoming fixated or stagnant in one of the trajectory stages signals a lack of growth on the part of the dad, child or both. Here, we want to focus on you. We've identified stages of being a dad as defined by the role we play and influence in the relationship with our child.

We four authors are active in marriage ministry and mentoring couples. Something we all agree on and regularly share with our married couples is that God the Father designed marriage to last forever, but our kids are a temporary assignment. Their natural growth arc would see them maturing from infant to youth and moving into an independent life as an adult. We as a dad have a parental responsibility to raise them up so that they acquire the education, social skills, emotional maturity and spiritual foundation to transition into a healthy adult phase. Regressing, oppressing or suppressing their trajectory for our selfish benefit is akin to parental neglect.

As fathers who grow, it's vital to understand that our evolution as dad also directly affects their maturation from child to adult. We are directly connected to their growth, and while we can create positive environments to foster that improvement, we also have the burden of knowing the detrimental side to our negative decisions and behaviors. This is why mirroring the model our Father God provides for us is so important in getting it right. Our kids only have one shot at getting their cognitive stages right. While we can lose a career and go back to school or find a new line of work, kids who missed out on earlier formative stages of development experience an absence of maturity or growth in those areas.

How can we help? Simple. You're Dad! Understanding your relationship stages as they are connected to your child will help you identify progress markers that signal you are on the right path toward raising your child up right and to the best of their potential.

> *Train up a child in the way he should go,*
> *And when he is old he will not depart from it.*
> Proverbs 22:6 (NKJV)

There is absolute truth in this popular Scripture. What is often missed is the gap of time between training them up as a child and their returning to the foundational roots when they are old. The time in between is usually what we might refer to as pre-adolescence, adolescence, puberty, late teen and into early adulthood. Of course this doesn't suggest that your child is limited or locked into these natural life stages, but as a general rule biology, physiology and psychology play dominant roles that influence your child's behavior.

## The Dad Curve

From the angst of pre-teens to the struggle to break free as an independent adult, our kids will progress through smooth times as well as times where we might not like the way they behave very much. Although you might feel as though you've lost touch with your child for a season, God the Father assures you that the investment you made during their childhood was not in vain.

Equally important to understanding your child's maturation cycle, is showing you how to progress through your own parental trajectory in a way to best influence them in theirs. We will share what we refer to as the Dad Curve that consist of five stages that are directly mutual to you and your child.

What makes them unique from our own personal life's trajectory is that the Dad Curve is interdependent upon you and your child just as the spiritual walk toward salvation and sanctification is interdependent upon you and God the Father. One without the other makes the Dad Curve impossible. Let's take a look.

## Stage 1 – Provider / Protector Dad

*13 Be watchful, stand firm in the faith, act like men, be strong. 14 Let all that you do be done in love.*
1 Corinthians 16:13-14 (ESV)

Do you recall the day your bundle of joy came into this world? If you're like us, there was a powerful mix of emotions ranging from joy, fear, happiness, worry, uncertainty and so many other feelings swirling around like crazy through our hearts and heads, but one thing that was rock-solid was that we'd protect that little package of sweetness come hell or high water. We would've ripped through steel to fight Goliath himself if that was what it would take to keep baby safe.

Maybe you also felt the pinch of finances immediately getting tighter as diapers, formula and day care began to consume every extra penny. Working overtime, extra jobs or even a complete career change became your way of making your passion to provide possible. The provider/protector ethos is a natural occurrence. It's rooted in our alpha's biological construction as a way of protecting the species and ensuring the continuation of our family line.

This stage is also a temporary one that evolves into the Authoritarian Stage as your child grows older and requires structure more than Pampers. It is during this first stage when you begin to form the foundational relationship that shapes both of your future growth arcs. Dads can be prone to remaining in the provider stage as a way to show love, and sometimes control over their child. Buying material items becomes more important than giving time, attention and love. Stagnation at this early cycle has a high potential for suppressing progress along the healthy Dad Curve and leaving your child feeling like yet another possession instead of a cherished person.

The best way to counter you desire to clutch onto this stage is understanding stewardship. Most people first think of giving money when they hear the word stewardship, but that's limiting the potential for experiencing an unlimited opportunity for freedom, receiving and blessings. Our cars, cash and kids are gifts from God. So is our marriage, home, health and everything we experience. The way we treat the gift is a reflection of the way we feel about the gift giver. No wonder we trashed our kid brother's birthday present as a child, or maybe still today!

Our children belong to God. He entrusted us with them for a season, and to cling onto them while lording provision or protection (potentially dominance) over them is to snuff the potential joy out of God's gift. Simply put, we are blessed with the gift of caring for God's gift. Part of that stewardship is allowing the gift (your child) to mature through the stages until actualizing the stage of their own adulthood. Don't use your provisions as a carrot on a stick or as a means to show your love. Provide and protect them in a way that allows for their natural growth into the next stage.

## Stage 2 – Authoritarian Dad

*Whoever spares the rod hates their children, but the one who loves their children is careful to discipline them.*
Proverbs 13:24 (NIV)

Moving from one stage in the Dad Curve to the next doesn't mean that the attributes from your previous one disappears, but that it's time to add structure atop the solid foundation you've laid in the past effort. This stage surfaces once your child begins needing rules over rocking. That's not to say we can't still snuggle with the little bugger, but as humans tend to go, we require structure and order to maintain a straight path toward becoming fully actualized.

Laying down the law isn't going to turn your kid against you. Let's go back to the beginning. We mean the very beginning. When God created creation, it required that He establish order out of chaos. How about we pitch a tent in Genesis 1:1-2 for a little bit.

*"In the beginning God created the heavens and the earth. The earth was formless and void, and darkness was over the surface of the deep, and the Spirit of God was moving over the surface of the waters."*
Genesis 1:1-2 (NASB)

How does this reflect the relationship you have or had with your child as you both progressed from the "Twinkle Twinkle Little Star" stage to the "Don't Stick the Cat's Tail in the Outlet" stage? Evolving from one posture in life to another can be very confusing. Not only because there's a child involved but because in the midst of change there can be disorganization and uncertainty. When you mirror the perfect dad, God the Father, you see how your actions shift the atmosphere.

By observing or watching carefully and deliberately, you're aware of your child's maturity and their need for order in what was once a rattling, rambling existence of naps and Goldfish Crackers. You are the one who has the authority to begin bringing order in your child's world. Our Father's example empowers you to act on His authority to behold authority over your child. Understanding the loving nature of God also helps you to temper that authority with love, understanding and light. Through His wisdom, you are able to hover over what was once chaos and proclaim it is good.

Remember though, that this stage is a drastic shift from what once was cuddles and constant affirmation. Really, who doesn't want to be complimented for napping? But seriously, wade with caution into this stage with lots of patience, mercy and grace as to not overwhelm your child.

## Stage 3 – Mentor Dad

*Remember your leaders, who spoke the word of God to you. Consider the*
*outcome of their way of life and imitate their faith.*
Hebrews 13:7 (NIV)

We believe everyone needs a mentor and everyone needs to be mentored. Unfortunately, very few men have actually been mentored or know where to begin to start the process of mentoring. A wonderful piece of advice about why we actually mentor also comes with a caution. If we mentor our child to accomplish a set of our established check-off boxes in the process of being mentored, then upon completion of that process our child mirrors us. If instead we show them the love of God the Father as reflected from us, in the end they too will mirror God.

We'd like to reinforce the value of growing through the previous two stages to illustrate the importance of the progression for you and your child moving through the stages together. Moving into a mentoring stage will be tough if there's no initial bond or boundaries where your child sees you as their parent and authority. If that is lacking, there's nothing wrong with taking the time to solidify the previous stages. Now, we're not suggesting bottle feedings for the fourteen-year-old but showing uninhibited love and affirmation for them is always welcome at any age and stage.

While the child's chronological age affects their mental, physical and psychological ability to function, it doesn't mean that if you're in the process of restoring a lost or broken relationship all is lost. Provider/Protector and the Authoritarian can be established at all ages but will obviously look different while mending a prodigal relationship versus an infant. The beauty of mirroring God the Father's perfect example is that He is always willing and welcoming to a loving relationship. Don't throw in the towel if you have to backtrack a bit before pressing forward. We want to share a few tips for helping you along in mentoring your child to be like God the Father.

1. Integrity – We'll go back to the monkey see, monkey do simplicity of being a dad, but obviously, there is no monkeying around where being a man of integrity is involved. Just understand that you are in large part what your kids see you do.

2. Reliable – We often lose our credibility and witness by making promises we aren't able or capable of making good on. Maybe it's well-intentioned, but once a mentor makes a promise and fails to follow through, it's hard to rebound. You're not required to make promises or vows to you child, so be careful before you swear an oath that's not necessary or needed. Simply let your yes be yes and your no be no. Of course, you can say no.

3. Relatable – The beauty of being a mentor in your father-child relationship is that the bond between you both is already established. It's not like a cold-call at a social event or being introduced to someone in need of a guiding hand. You're Dad, but you still have to remain open and honest when conducting yourself as their mentor. It cannot always be do as I say and not as I do. The lessons you teach your child will more often be caught rather than taught.

4. Caring – Unless you show your child how to care for another person as well as care for themselves, they may flounder in that department. Boys to men are especially deficient in the areas of compassion. Where men miss that mark comes from the inability to empathize. The Latin root of the word compassion is to "co-suffer," or to feel as someone else feels. Men aren't the best at naturally sharing the expression of feelings, but once aware we can become better. We can also teach our kids what it means and feels like to care and be cared for.

5. Connecting – We learned there's a major difference between communicating and connecting with people. Most dads are great at talking. We talk about sports, work, politics, each other, just to name a few, but are we really connecting? Too often, we talk to our kid without speaking with them. Growing in your skill as dad requires learning

how to actually connect. Asking the right questions, active listening and observing not only what they say but how they say is are all part of making meaningful connections rather than simply batting words back and forth.

## Stage 4 - Friend Dad

*One who has unreliable friends soon comes to ruin,*
*but there is a friend who sticks closer than a brother.*
Proverbs 18:24 (NIV)

Periods of mentorship often create avenues for deep, intimate friendships. It would be tough to intentionally pour into someone's life without opening the doors for a relationship. That holds true in business mentoring as well as between you and your child. Of course, there should always have been a friendly component mixed in your relationship throughout each stage, but becoming friends develops more legitimately once your child reaches an age of maturity where independent decisions can be made in their lives and choices involving mutual bonding.

Growing into the friend stage we will also see that the previous postures of provider, protector, authoritarian and mentor have generally passed. We'll share a word of caution as it applies to the common occurrence of dominance. Too often dads refuse to relinquish control over the direction of their child's life. Either it's unintentional, overzealously wanting to guide them into what they feel is best or purposely maintaining a grip for the pleasure of controlling another person. None of these motives are healthy options when dealing with an independent, adult child. Instead, the goal of a dad who has also grown through the stages of their role in the child's life is to become less of a presence in the daily activity of the child as their child grows more capable and independent as an adult. A friendship bond represents more of a mutual respect and choice to share a close connection.

## Stage 5 – Peer Dad

*Iron sharpens iron, and one man sharpens another.*
Proverbs 27:17 ESV

The final evolution along the Dad Curve is becoming a peer. Does that sound weird? Well, it's a completely natural progression in the life-relationship cycle between a dad and child. Common bonds such as your child having their own kids, a career, home and adult life just like you set you both on level ground. Of course, you'll always be dad, but the interaction shifts as their life looks more and more like yours. It's not even uncommon to go into business together as partners and peers.

Studies show that as dads and their children age, the health of their relationships affect the well-being of both parties in critical ways. Dads experienced elevated depressive symptoms while involved in a negative relationship with their child. A negative connection between dad and daughter often saw increased symptoms between both.

Peer relationships can make the challenges of a maturing dad-to-child relationship an easier transition as both gain new perspectives and experiences through time. For your child to continue to relate to you in a subservient posture when they've reached adulthood requires them to deny their own identity and independence. Honoring you as the father is not the same as relating to you as Daddy when they are also a mom or dad. That honor comes from intentionally giving you respect, authority and position in their life as their dad because they choose to, not because they have to.

The growth into a peer relationship can actually intensify the intimacy between dad and child as each person no longer views the other in a one-dimensional perspective as simply dad or child. Realizing that we're both multi-faceted adults brings about new opportunities for connecting in areas other than family ties. Think back to your own experiences with your parents. When did you first realize they actually had a life that involved more than being your mom and dad?

The best and maybe funniest way to describe that first realization of being peers is like the first time you saw your teacher at the grocery store. Understanding that your lives no longer revolve around each other can be a hard truth to accept, but in order to grow along the Dad Curve, it's something we must expect, accept and encourage. Soon, it'll become a relationship you deeply enjoy.

---

### George's Session:

Growing up in the home of a pastor there were certain life-giving rituals that will forever remain imprinted in my memory. One of those rituals was baby dedication Sundays. It was always exciting to see parents and grandparents stand in front of the congregation and publicly dedicate their children back to God and receive prayers of blessings in helping to raise and steward the gift that had been entrusted to them. In one sense it was the constant reminder to me as a kid growing up that parents don't have all the answers as they need divine assistance throughout the life of the child. In a much broader sense, it taught me that God the Father gives children to parents as gifts to steward and guide along life's journey. Not to own and control but to partner with God.

It was a surreal moment when we had our kids and my wife, and I took our place at the front of the altar dedicating our two back to God as his children and asking for his grace to parent and steward them well. Those times were very humbling because we knew we were so young and ill-equipped as parents that we would need all the help we could get! Especially from God.

I've grown a lot as a father since the beginning. I say this because my kids actually tell me I've grown. Somehow, they discerned I was faking it until I made it. Meaning I had not walked the path of being a father of one kid let alone two, and I've struggled at times with all the stages of the Dad Curve. Fatherhood has been both rewarding and a challenge at the same time. The most rewarding part has been seeing the fruit of my labor, prayers and guidance in the lives of my adult children.

The Bible teaches us *"Children are a heritage from the Lord, offspring a reward from him. Like arrows in the hands of a warrior are children born in one's youth"* (Psalms 127:4-5). I love this verse because every man and father sees himself as a warrior. We all want to be like *Gladiator* or *Braveheart* protecting, providing, conquering and winning the day in the lives of our wife and kids. And yet this verse points out that it's not about how well we fight to conquer our kids or dominate their will or die trying to win every battle. The goal of fathering is always and has always been how well we shoot them like arrows into their destiny and life's calling. It's about our stewardship of preparing them to live a fruitful and productive life.

A few of the best questions that I learned to ask my kids that helped me grow and develop as a dad was, "How am I doing as a father?" or "How can I improve as a dad?" It takes a lot of humility and desire to grow to ask those questions to your kids. A lot. However, it takes courage to listen to their hearts when some of the things that they actually say might not be so flattering to your ego. In general, as dads we mostly think we do things the "right way" and we are the best at what we do. But our kids can be a pretty good gauge as to how well we are actually doing.

Throughout my kids' adolescent years, they both have given me some pretty good feedback. At times, it was how I could be a better listener and not try to fix everything? Ouch! Or they needed me as a dad to understand them in the current moments of vulnerability and frustrations and not try to teach them some big life lesson every chance I got. Other times they pointed out my tone at moments was not the best and sometimes they felt like I prioritized other things before them. But with every list of examples of how I could improve as a dad, they generally ended the list with the sentiment that I was a great dad. Not because I did everything right. But because I had a heart to improve and grow as a dad.

### Richard's Session:

To know is to grow. If we don't deal and get real, we can't heal. I am writing the truth to give hope to you, Dad. I've seen fathers, me included, that didn't know what being a man looked like. It's okay to say that it's okay to not know how. It's not okay to do nothing about it, though. There are many things I don't know how to do. I can't fly a plane; I can't base jump and I can't scuba dive. Guess what? There's good news because if I really wanted to do any of those things, there are, classes, teachers, instructors and proven processes that will enable me to accomplish them.

That's what we did and at first, I was not on board, but don't miss the opportunity. Do it now. Do something on purpose. Yes, there was a time I was looking around watching another failing marriage transpire, but this time I said enough is enough, I can't live like this anymore. I thought it was going to be easy to just receive God and go about my new life, my new walk. I thought it was going to be simple and it was. It just wasn't easy.

Getting involved with church and men's groups were very eye-opening to me. I did Quest for Authentic, I did the Ed Cole Maximize Manhood and was issued an awesome sword upon my certificate of completion, which took a year. We were volunteering in pre-marriage classes, we were teaching marriage classes, and we were reading all kinds of books together as a couple. We'd also surrounded ourselves with people and friends wanting the same things in marriage and parenting. Our friends, Dave and Ashley Willis with MarriageToday, say before you take advise or counsel from anyone, they have to have four things.

They have to love God.

They have to love you.

They have to love your spouse.

And they have to love your marriage.

I believe this to be solid marriage and parenting advise. I have seen too many marriages end in divorce because husbands are siding and listening to their mothers instead of their wives. When I say many, I mean many. It's okay to love your mom, but dads, a momma's boy has to die 100%. You are no longer tied to your mother's apron.

*"Therefore shall a man leave his father and mother, and shall cleave to his wife and the two shall become one flesh.*
Genesis 2:24

You see, as men we have to take responsibility for all of the areas of our life where we have done wrong. Doing this is an act of humility.

You are able to say you're sorry and mean it. Also I would like to say if you know your parents were less than perfect, they were probably hanging on by a thread themselves. I am so thankful that even though my adult children separated themselves from me for a season, I was able to step back and accept my part although my heart was hurting. It helped me extend grace at a time retaliation would have been justified by the world's standards. I just gave them space and prayed without ceasing.

I had faith and believed what I had learned. Bring them up in the way they shall go and when they get older they will not depart. After a few months everyone had a chance to breath, and we all started talking again. We deeply missed each other. I want to be the father that, when I'm gone from this earth, my children are rejoicing my life and not in my death.

*For if a man know not how to rule his own home, how shall he take care of the church of God?*
1st Timothy 3:5

Men whether you want to believe it or not you have to face the fact that it starts with you. Not your wife, your kids, your mom and dad, or your Granny Annie, but you. God made you a warrior and not a wuss. It's time to make a difference, to make a change.

As we kept going, I started to learn and change lifelong bad habits that were impossible before knowing Jesus. I really hope by now you can see through all of us that God is the great redeemer, the great healer, the chain breaker, the way maker. No matter what obstacle comes my way—and believe me brothers sometimes they are daily—I turn to my Father for His guidance.

What circle of life are we putting our hope in? The world's circle that brings death? Or God's circle that brings life? Brother, make no mistake here. You are serving a master right now as you read this. Here's the truth: you can't serve two masters. You must serve one or the other. If you are not living your life for Christ, then you're living your life for Satan. Even if you say you're a pretty good guy, you haven't broken any laws, you love your family and you try to make people feel good about themselves. Yeah, that is serving the killer of your soul.

I'm not trying to make you angry with me, I'm trying to get you to think in a climate and culture that does all the thinking for us. We are a creation; we must think to create. To love means to fight; fight the enemy of our soul. The only power Satan has is the power we give him, because he is not equal to God in any means. God changes our heart over time as we grow our faith. If God can heal the blind, cure the sick and bring the dead back to life, then you are no match to the healing coming your way.

Press in now, call your wife who wants a divorce, call your children you haven't spoken to, or parents who are estranged. Life is clicking by so fast these days. I want my children when they read this book to say wow, I didn't know everything my family was going through but I see now everything my Dad did to try and give us a life worth living. Even if they don't, I will still continue to search for a peace that only God can give us.

### Juan's Session:

I guess I have to echo my co-author, Richard Bright with the statement of, "I did not know what a man was, I was never developed, and this is an important thing to do." Earlier you read that understanding your relationship stages as they are connected to your child will help you identify progress markers that signal you are on the right path toward raising your child up right and to the best of their potential.

*Train up a child in the way he should go,*
*And when he is old he will not depart from it.*
Proverbs 22:6 (NKJV)

This is so important as we develop our children and help them see their identity in Christ; teach them to respect the authority of our position as dad and help them discover their spiritual gifts so that they grow in maturity. Our goal as dad should be to prepare our kids so when they step into adulthood, they're living a fulfilled life in Christ and also working in the gifting that God has freely given them.

I never understood any of that until I met Jesus Christ. It wasn't until I came to know God the Father that I experienced growth in His kingdom. After ten years of being incarcerated and twenty-six years of addictions, I was saved at thirty-six years old. Since then, God has blessed me with an incredible marriage to Ruthy and complete restoration with my family, planting Get Wrapped Church, We Are Heavicans clothing line, a first-time homeowner, book author, podcaster and radio talk show host.

God's been so good to me and I believe we're only getting started. I share this to say that no matter where you are in life or how old you are, do not ever quit. You have the opportunity to change everything for the better by accepting Jesus Christ as your savior.

It's time for you to grow into the father and leader God created you to be. Here's something you can do to start growing. Identify some of the lies that have been leading you into destruction. How a man deals with problems in life says a lot about his character. Is your character grounded in God the Father? We need a generation of Godly men who will lead their kids like God the Father.

Growing as dads also allows us to become great fathers not just for our home, but to help the fatherless become acquainted with their heavenly Father. Today as a pastor, I get to father many who don't have dads. Pastor Tom Lane said a father will not be a fully effective leader and teacher to his children without acknowledging God in the entire process of life.

**Scott's Session:**

When Leah and I were first married and in the mix of mashing our families together, I thought I had fatherhood all figured out. I'd approach it the same way I succeeded throughout my career. In law enforcement, I'd held a command position since 1992. That's a long time to be a supervisor in such high-risk and dangerous positions, but it came naturally, and I enjoyed it. The problem was kids aren't highly trained undercover agents or SWAT operators.

Because it was what I knew, it was what I relied on. I focused on keeping them in line, which to me was akin to showing them love by making sure they were safe. The reality is, I didn't know how to grow beyond what only made me comfortable. All of the kids were having to shuck and jive just to make sure they complied with my expectations.

I know we all had great times, but those times came at the expense of functioning within my rules and regulations. I'm aware enough to understand that a rigid environment wasn't the best foundation for the relationship with the kids, but I wasn't sure how else to relate to them other than the way my subordinates operated around me at work.

As I focused on fathering the way God is a dad to me, I realized the value of growth in the way I related to the kids. Sure, our kids need to be protected and provided for but once they've learned the purpose of order, it was my time to progress toward deepening our connections through mentoring. After I relaxed a bit and stopped worrying they'd do something to hurt themselves or one of the other kids, the connections for molding their hearts and minds toward a relationship with God took priority.

As the kids have matured, I've found my role in their lives has remained important but different. I focus on their making wise and thoughtful independent actions. Leah and I both make sure that each kid focuses more and more on Christ as they've grown a little less reliant upon us for everything.

Dad, it's okay to let go. God did not intend for our kids to be a permanent assignment. Our mark of doing the job of being dad right is to teach them to become capable adults. Their growth potential depends on your growth acceptance. Allow their ability to mature toward independence to serve as affirmation of a job well done. What I'm experiencing now is that, while the relationship with our college age kids looks zero like it did at childhood, it has evolved into a loving peer connection. Of course, there's always a time and place where even the most independent kid needs Daddy.

# FATHERS WHO BUILD LEGACIES

*"Obedience is the password that unlocks destiny and fulfillment!"*
Pastor Adam McCain

When we discuss legacy building, the first things that usually come to mind are savings accounts, investment portfolio, cash gifts, property and real estate. Basically, money, money, and more money. We think in temporal, materialistic terms for securing the generational memory of what our life on earth meant. We think that's why so many dads feel like failures when it comes to considering legacy building. Lacking a vast entrepreneurial empire, dads wave the white flag of surrender before truly realizing the short-sighted nature of a misguided understanding of what constitutes a father's legacy.

We'd like to introduce you to a never-ending wealth which produces value for a thousand generations. Sorry, but it's not a Wall Street insider's information or a hot tip for quick cash. We're talking about obedience. Obedience you might ask with a skeptical furrow of your brow. Yes, your obedience is the key to legacy.

*⁵ You shall not bow down to them or worship them; for I, the Lord your God, am a jealous God, punishing the children for the sin of the parents to the third and fourth generation of those who hate me, ⁶ but showing love to a thousand generations of those who love me and keep my commandments.*
*Exodus 20:5-6 (NIV)*

Dads have the power to continue generational legacies, both good and bad dependent upon their willingness to be obedient. They also have the authority to interrupt them.

## Breaking Bad Legacies

A destructive curse can stop right now, with you. Let's take a step back before going forward. It's vital that you truly understand the historical and biblical significance of these examples. While there are numerous examples of fathers failing their sons, there are also encouraging illustrations of fathers fulfilling their God-ordained role.

We want to encourage you that, even if your dad had failed to establish a standard of strong legacy building, there is still hope for you. That hope is found in God the Father. Old Testament hero Abraham, who was previously known as Abram was cursed with a horrible father, Terah. He was described as a wicked man who believed in many gods and created idols to sell.

Terah even tried to have Abram murdered when Nimrod threw the boy into a fiery furnace because Abram opposed his father's wicked influence. God protected His son. Despite a failed past, Abraham went on to become a mighty man and the father of many nations. Men, we are still being called by our heavenly Father to be the men He first created us to be. It doesn't matter what the relationship with your dad looked like. It's a curse, but not an excuse. The curse can be broken by relying on God the Father to save you, the way He did for Abram.

## Losing A Good Legacy

You are being offered the opportunity to proclaim a new beginning if the legacy you're currently living in is not one based on obedience. An example of losing what was intended to be an unending legacy that would remain intact until Jesus Christ returned to establish His kingdom on earth was that of King Saul. We're very familiar with the Bible's King David, but he wasn't the first earthly king of God's people.

Saul was selected by God as His people's first king, and that meant his legacy would've reigned until Christ's triumphant return. Actually, the Messiah (Jesus) would've come from the line of Saul had he embraced his anointing and royal legacy. It was Saul's rebellion against God through disobedience that cost him not only the throne, but every generation to follow him an abundant legacy.

Conversely, it was David's loving obedience that led to his being blessed with a legacy that includes not only the blood line within which Jesus was born, but also the royal authority by which Jesus proclaimed the legal, natural king heirship. David's fatherly legacy is no different than the blessings God the Father is waiting to bestow upon you. You and every generation after you have the potential for living the blessed life within God's undying love.

**Personal Legacy Shifts**

We authors have each personally experienced the legacy created by dads. One of us, George, had a father's legacy passed on to him by his dad, who served the Lord for many years before passing away to join God the Father. Richard, Juan and Scott each chose to break past legacies of abuse, abandonment and generations apart from God by obediently submitting themselves to the Father.

If you can look back across multiple generations of God-fearing men in your bloodline, then thank God for you. If you are like so many other men and can only look back across broken pieces and spiritual disobedience, then do not fear. You can be the one who breaks the cycle as well as the one who rights the path for yourself, your child and every generation to follow. You want to talk about being a superhero to your kid; start the legacy of obedience and break open the promises of heaven that will pour out for thousands of generations to follow you.

**Non-Blood Legacy**

In an earlier chapter, we honored fathers who love beyond biology and shared the example of Jesus being raised by his stepfather, Joseph. Yes, even non-biological dads can break old generational cycles of defeat and ignite a new legacy of obedient victory. In addition to Joseph, we love looking at Moses's father-in-law, Jethro. Moses was separated from his biological dad at an early age and raised up in a pagan home. His call by God into ministry service was affirmed by the most direct dad-like relationship he had experienced in Jethro. It was Jethro's fatherly activation of Moses's anointing (Exodus 4:18) that set him off along his path toward claiming his destiny in God through obedience to the Father.

Not only did Moses enjoy a fruitful legacy as the father of nations, but Jethro's obedience to God's desire also allowed him to enjoy that same legacy. There are many examples of men surrendering their hearts, heads and hobbies to the will of God. Their reward wasn't an easy life, material riches or job promotions. They were more valuable with an eternal return of gains on the dad's investment of obedience as they single-handedly gifted their family with a legacy enmeshed in God's love.

Legacy in the most basic of definitions is the handing down of something from those who have gone before you. This is where we trip up on the notion of handing down material wealth, diamonds, property and prestige. Let's commit to move beyond the trap of man's definition and step into the supernatural understanding of legacy from a spiritual realm that does not rot in the rain, depreciate in value or bankrupt depending on stocks.

We want to offer ten tips to legacy building:

1. Caught Not Taught – Our kids watch us for key clues and indicators for defining their own lives as well as whether what you say reconciles with what you do. Your legacy will be caught in your actions. Your legacy will be passed down by the way they see you live.

2. Purposeful – Pursue life with passion and intentionality. That doesn't mean you must conquer every challenge, but it does mean that your kids will experience your vigor for life by the way you approach it.

3. Love – We've shared 1 Corinthians 16:13-14 because that is one of the best ways of living out the legacy of your life. Be the dad. Be the husband. Be the man. But always do everything in love.

4. Write – Although many people talk about writing the next great novel or simply trying their hand at crafting a good adventure, learning to document our observations, thoughts, dreams and joys is a great gift that helps cement your legacy.

5. History – Set the backstory to your legacy by sharing stories of your family's past. If you are breaking a disobedient cycle and charting the new generational course, then make sure your child knows about the prior darkness, so they'll better appreciate the new light.

6. Straight Path – Be very clear in the vision for your legacy. That also includes truthfulness and transparency about whether you are continuing an incredible legacy set in motion decades before or if you are the first positive link in an obedient chain going forward. Let honesty be a tenant of your legacy.

7. Cause Above Circumstance – Establishing your family's legacy in God's Word above personal or emotional feelings about needing a change will lay a sound foundation upon which growth will rest.

8. Present – There's a saying that sums this up: "Let your presence be their presents." While younger kids may prefer packages of gifts, the truth is, you are a gift and your actually being with your child is the greatest gift they will ever receive.

9. I Am Second – Ground your legacy in doing for others. Jesus set the example when He shared that He came to serve and not be served. Allow your child to experience your humanity by placing the needs of others above your own.

10. Vision Casting – Don't leave your child to guess what you would've wanted them to do in tough situations. Speak open and often about your vision and understanding of the legacy you are creating for them. Make sure that even once you are gone, the assurance of what

you continued or started is planted deep in their spirit so they too will grow to continue your gift of legacy.

**Specific Legacy**

Speaking in terms of materialistic legacy, giftings can be easier because it involves tangible items such as bank accounts, property deeds, car titles or cash transactions. We may tend to avoid true, generational legacy listing because it seems abstract. Unless it's something we can count, crush or carry, we tend to avoid it. Instead of ending this chapter with fuzzy feelings about eternal legacy building as something to only think or pray about, try writing it out in specific concrete terms.

What do you want your wife, child, family and friends to say about you once you've passed away: "He played a mean game of golf?" What they'll say should be a direct connection to the legacy you've established. Write out what you value, your views on walking and serving in faith, the love you want to share and be shared, how you want to treat others and in turn have them treat people, describe your style of open communications with loved ones, and detail the actions that you deem necessary for living a life worthy of emulation.

This is serious business. Can you even imagine that what you write down today may serve as a family legacy blueprint that's passed down to generations for a thousand years? Why wouldn't it be? You are taking the dad responsibility for your family's pathway. You wouldn't drive them into the brick wall of a favorite restaurant on purpose, so why would you not provide prayer-inspired directions for living a blessed and worthy legacy life? It is your shoulders upon which every generation of your family is going to stand, so make sure they are strong, square and sturdy. That's what dads are for!

---

**Juan's Session:**

As I'm sure you've guessed by now, before I accepted Jesus Christ as my lord and savior, I was a horrible dad. I'm not proud of that but I know that it's part of my testimony. I also feel that if you're in a place where you've beaten yourself up over past failures as a father, you need to know that it's not too late.

Once I came to know God, I also learned what it was to have a Father and grew into what it meant to actually *be* a father. God fully restored the relationship with all of my kids. Actually, they all now live in Texas and we see each other all of the time.

I wish I could say everything is just perfect, it's not, but it gets a lot better every day, every week and every year. It's a lifetime process. In that process you have to change who you are in order to change what you do. Real change requires a heart change. What you have today is out of the things you did in the past, and the beauty of that is what you start doing today will change your tomorrow. Don't waste today because it's not too late to make the effort.

Remember, your children are like gardens, and the seeds you sow into them will grow and you'll reap the benefits. A financial inheritance is temporary, but heavenly wisdom is eternal. The best investment you can give your children is Godly examples in teaching them about the importance of character, values, and beliefs. These lessons will not only change them, but also everyone they come in contact with will benefit. Especially their families.

Here're a few things I do to prioritize legacy building in my life. I have daily morning quiet time with God to learn to hear His voice in the quiet place, so you know what it sounds like when it gets chaotic. I also prioritize my wife. Ruthy is my everything and I will be married to her for the rest of my life, no matter what. I also prioritize going to church, telling the truth, working hard for my family, but never loving money more than God. I will be an example at home first, then to others. I have realized that, although I have made every mistake as a father and as a son, I can choose to be there now. Every one of these actions are helping my children to see what life is like with God.

We build a legacy by continually working on becoming a family. The question is, what legacy do you want to leave your family?

### Richard's Session:

I have truly been so blessed to have been able to write this book with these friends of mine. I think by now after reading everything in this book, you have come to the realization that we are building legacies. You might have started this journey many moons ago or you might be starting right now, but Dad, what legacy do you want to leave behind? A verse that sticks out to me now, which back in my drinking days I couldn't care less about, is the scripture below.

*"A good man leaves an inheritance to his children's children.*
Proverbs 13:22

I used to think I needed to try and build my squandered wealth back. I'd spent more money on booze, drugs and pornography than I care to admit. I often wonder if I could get the money back how much would it have been. Probably over five hundred thousand, I bet. I hear about pastors or people who just had a great life with no major problem ever. I used to think what a boring life. Now I think what a marvelous life. That life is too late for me. Sure my life is great now, but I wish I didn't have to go through so much.

My kids have been through some stuff too, and they are all so brilliant. I could not be prouder of our three children. I love them so dearly. One day I will be blessed with grandbabies and we intend to love them as much as possible. I already love them more than they will probably ever know, because I'm praying that they will never see any of the hurts that could have been avoided.

I pray that the legacy I leave my grandchildren is the high road, the road less traveled. Not the wide road that most of us who are lost somehow end up on. Sure, it would be nice to leave a monetary inheritance, but a spiritual inheritance I have learned pays far better dividends. Can you picture your children, grandchildren or great-grandchildren turning to Jesus for their answers instead of picking up addictions they were never meant to carry in the first place?

I'm just so sorry that it has taken me so long to figure how wonderful and beautiful the Word of God is. I'm still learning daily. I get another day to make things better in my life, to grow and change into the man

God created me to be, the husband my wife is longing for. A father my children will turn to just to have a relationship with, kinda like God wants from us now. He just wants us to talk to Him, to tell Him about our lives. All the great accomplishments as well as all the issues that bind us up. He just wants to hear our voices.

*"If my people who are called by my name humble themselves, and pray and seek my face and turn from there wicked ways, then I will hear them from heaven and will forgive their sin and heal their land."*
2 Chronicles 7:14

Not sure about you and the horse you road in on, but as for me and my saddle sores, I could use the healing of my land. Healing our lands must first start with God healing our hearts. You see, it's not all your spouse's fault, and it's not all of your children's fault, nor is it everyone else's fault. Sure they may have played a significant role but that is because God needs to heal their land too. This vicious circle only makes sense when we see that when we are disconnected from our life support, we will die. That life support is Jesus Christ.

When we think of what God means, we need to think of Christ crucified. All of our insecurities are covered by the blood of Christ. You have to believe that when we look at ourselves and see all the sin we are draped in, God sees His son's atoning sacrifice that has made us white and pure as snow.

The issue we struggle with is we can't see it, because if we did we would feel His love and the price He paid. This price was a ransom for your soul. When I think of this price, it helps me want to get closer to my heavenly Father. I want to do better, I want to do right, I want to live right for the first time in my life. That was my feeling when I realized the message of the cross.

I pray you'll decide to take this journey with us. One man at a time helping another man to liberate his soul for Jesus. How do you build a mighty man? This simple, one verse at a time followed by one prayer at a time process. My marriage was healed when my wife and I started praying together. This is an intimacy that goes much further than a bedroom could ever build. This was a petition of my heart to know and love my wife as the gift God gave me. How can I go to God and ask Him to hear any prayer if I cannot see my wife as His gift to me?

*"He who finds a wife finds a good thing and receives favor from the Lord"*
Proverbs 18:22

Men we don't even have to ask, because we are given favor by the Lord. Guys our wives are a good thing. Let's help each other move in a direction that gives glory to God. Let's put away the wrong ways we learned and open our heart to a new way. A way that is freedom and a way that is life giving itself. I never thought that God would take my ashes and turn them to beauty, I never thought my life could be addiction free, I never thought my marriage would be saved, I never thought we would do comedy on a stage for thousands, I never thought I would travel the world doing conferences in His name, I never thought I would ever read a book much less write one. What have you never?

It's your legacy to create and leave for your family.

### George's Session:

As you can tell by now, my father left a rich legacy behind. He knew he only had one chance to make a difference in this world. As a son, I am certainly grateful he did not waste his one chance. As great as he was as a father and friend, he did not just wake up and his legacy just magically appeared. It took time and consistency. He even knew there were others who had gone before him who helped him leave something of significance behind. He was not just a giver of a legacy but a receiver of a broader legacy that was bigger than himself.

Let me give you a fuller picture.

My father would often say, "Without God you can do nothing," based on one of his favorite passages in John 15. He knew the giver of life and creation was the giver of all good things. Daily he thanked God for everything, especially his Son Jesus that sacrificed his life to pay for our sins. For him, his life's work and legacy were directly tied back to the old rugged cross and empty grave. Every day my father worked for God's kingdom as a pastor and lover of people. He knew he was an imperfect husband, father and pastor. Yet he knew the perfect Father that gave us his perfect Son. If my father were to leave anything of a legacy on earth, he knew it started with the legacy and inheritance of God's grace.

My grandfather was just as much of a lover of God, family and people as my Dad. My father learned how to be a good father as he looked to the example of my grandfather. In fact, still to this day I can walk in my hometown and meet someone my grandfather impacted by his life and legacy, and they would remember how kind and compassionate he was to all. How he loved his family and how devoted he was to his children and grandchildren. I am a part of a rich legacy of godly family men. When my Dad was in his last stages of ALS and in hospice care, one of the nurses pulled me to the side and reminded me of what a rich heritage I came from having such gifts for a grandfather and father. Even on my father's deathbed I was reminded that my father's legacy was not his own.

And just like every good steward of God's gifts, my father knew the legacy that he received from Christ and my grandfather could not stop there. Although imperfect, he tried to live his life as an example to everyone, but especially to his wife and kids. He had his shortcomings and rough edges as a family man but his impact and legacy lives on. You see, each of my father's children are all pastors and ministers just like dear old dad. Some say it's the family business. How many fathers can say their example paved the way for all of their kids to follow in their footsteps?

Like the branches of a family tree that tell the story of many generations of the past, I've begun to follow in the footsteps of my Dad and grandfather by creating my own family branches. While I too am an imperfect dad, I look to the grace of our perfect Father for his patience and guidance as I continue to steward my family and leave a legacy.

No matter where you are on your journey as a dad, it's not too late to start thinking of your legacy and what you will leave behind. You will be remembered in one way or another. The big question is how will your family and the world remember you and your legacy?

**Scott's Session:**

Talking about legacy can be a daunting task. It's often derailed because we focus on an intangible future event or occurrence that we assume can be set in motion today. That puts so much pressure on the effort of legacy building that most dads refuse to even wade into the waters. Let me encourage you that it is an effort well worth the work. And, for the sake of clarity, we don't dictate future events or directly control anyone else's lives long after we're gone.

Legacy building can begin today, but by first looking at the reality of future forecasting, this Scottish proverb usually proves true; "The best laid plans of mice and men often go astray." What this tells me is that we need to chill out and stop worrying about the future. God the Father has that under control. We can, though, lay the foundations that foster the potential for powerful legacies to grow.

Although talk about legacies usually centers around money, I focus on eternal gifts that will best benefit our kids and future generations. I'm not much at thinking in abstract concepts, so when it came time to develop serious plans for my family's legacy, I focused on the current process of laying a solid foundation. Before starting on my foundation I had to deal with the rocky soil from my own past. Without "working my dirt" I knew I was dooming my kids to the failed generational cycles of failure and dysfunction.

Leah and I both spent time focusing on our respective families' pasts. As we were aware, there was divorce, adultery, abandonment, addictions and so much more tracked back for decades. When we dug deeper, we were shocked at the depth of pain and darkness both of our family trees had produced. You see, everyone produces fruit. Some of that fruit is negative and born out of years of hurt, while others produce positive, life affirming fruit thanks to having God the perfect Father at the center of their family orchard.

I knew soul ties and strongholds from my family had to be confessed, forgiven and healed. Generations long before I arrived on the scene had to be forgiven for their actions that set a crooked path for a painful legacy. We do have the supernatural authority to right that path. We also have the God-ordained responsibility to never return to that route by remaining on God's straight and narrow path. Not only do we benefit from walking in obedience to God's loving will, but we give our kids and all future generations the potential for remaining a family focused on God the perfect Father.

Speaking of the Father, the most important legacy building gift you can give your child is introducing them to God. It's because of God that I was able to free myself from the shackles of my past and it's thanks to Him that I have the assurance of my kids being covered by His grace and blessings.

There's no assurance in money, investments or real estate. What you monetarily pass on might temporarily gain in earnings, but it will never survive eternity. No money on earth will spare your beloved child from suffering the generational curses of your life and the past your family dropped on your doorstep. But shining God's light so that your child sincerely desires to know the Father as they've seen Him exhibited through you is the greatest legacy you can give. And guess what? It costs you nothing but love, and that's a price we dads should all be willing to pay.

# ACKNOWLEDGMENTS

From George Gregory:

First thanks to God Almighty as without Him I could do nothing. Then to my beloved parents, the late Henry A. Gregory Jr. and Coleen H. Gregory, for giving me life and always believing in me.

Last but certainly not least, special thanks to my beautiful wife Tondra and awesome children Jaylen and Camryn for always pushing me to be my best self and for allowing me the ability to dream big, make makes and step outside the box.

———

From Juan Martinez:

I want to start by thanking my beautiful wife Ruthy. My Baby RUTH, you are a treasure, thank you for always believing in me. I also want to thank my children Jay, Nina and Jonathan for giving me another chance at being their dad.I want to thank Scott for always pushing me and for putting together this amazing book, you're a great example of a Kingdom man. Get Wrapped Church for always being so supportive.

## From Scott Silverii

A forever Thank You goes to my wife, Leah who I love and adore. Our kids continue to be blessings beyond belief. A huge shout out goes to our team at Five Stones Press, and last but never least my kingdom Brothers and co-authors; Richard, Juan and George. I love you and respect you. Thanks for agreeing to take this journey with me.

Richard is a dad of three and with his wife, Sheri, are comedians and entertaining speakers helping couples put fun and inspiration back in their relationships.

They share their humorous and transparent stories at churches, couples date night events and marriage conferences across the U.S.

They are the founders of Brighter Marriage a 501(c)(3) ministry.

George Gregory is the official Chaplain for the Los Angeles Chargers of the National Football League. Prior to moving to the Los Angeles area, George assisted the New York Jets and New York Giants for six seasons by providing marital support, seminars, retreats, pre-marriage and marriage counseling, and mentorship. For over a decade, he has been life and marriage coaching hundreds of professional athletes, coaches and their families.

George, and his wife Tondra, have been married for 25 years and have two children - Jaylen and Camryn. They are the founders of Journey for Life, a marriage ministry dedicated to equipping and educating couples on their journey to have successful relationships and marriages. They pastored regional churches for 20 years on the East Coast. While living in New York City, they planted a church on the Upper East Side of Manhattan.

George received his Master of Divinity degree from Duke Divinity School.

He has spoken several times on Trinity Broadcasting Network (TBN) in New York City, as well as invited guest speakers at Saddleback Church, Gateway Church, Marriage Today's XO Conference, the NBA All Star Breakfast, the NBA Legends Conference and the Professional Athletes Outreach.

Website - https://journeyforlifenow.org

YouTube - https://www.youtube.com/journeyforlife

IG - @georgeagregory @journeyforlifenow

Facebook - @journeyforlifenow

Juan Martinez is the founder of Wrapped in the Love of Christ Ministry and Love Live Lead Ministries and serves as the senior pastor of the Get Wrapped Church in Spring, Texas. Since 2010, the ministry has seen thousands of people say yes to Christ. Juan's heart and main focus is simply winning souls by wrapping them in the *love of Christ*.

Through dynamic ministering of the Word of God, Juan is a true revivalist with a burning *passion* and a deep desire to see the lost saved, the broken mended, the afflicted healed, and the body of Christ operate in its God-given authority.

God has transformed him from having a killing, stealing, and destroying mentality to a seed-sowing mindset, spreading the Good News to all who will listen. He has seen God move miraculously in his life and has a hunger for all of creation to experience the same.

Additionally, Juan is involved in speaking at various conferences and has appeared on many televised programs, and is the author of the Beyond The Yellow Brick Road: Unlocking the Promises of God.

Juan and his wife, Ruthy, have six children: Janina, Valery, Jonathan, Jay, Johnathan, and Joshua.

From left to right Jonathan, Josh, Valery, Me, Baby Ruth, Johnathan, Jay and Janina

We Are Heavicans- www.Heavicans.com
This Is Real Radio - www.juanmartinez.tv
Podcast - https://podcasts.subsplash.com/m3bb5k3/podcast.rss
Get Wrapped Church - www.getwrapped.tv

facebook.com/juanmartinez.tv
instagram.com/lovewinsu
youtube.com/ThisIsRealWithJuanMartinez

Dr. Scott Silverii's highly-decorated law enforcement career promptly ended when God called him out of public service and into HIS service. The "Chief" admits that leading people to Christ is more exciting than the twelve years he spent working undercover, sixteen years in SWAT command and five years as chief of police combined.

Scott has earned a Master of Public Administration and a Ph.D. in Cultural Anthropology with post-doctoral hours at The King's University seminary.

The author of 45 books, God led Scott into the digital ministry field where he and his wife, Leah, founded Five Stones Press, a Christian publishing house and Five Stones Church.Online. His work with faith-based writers with a heart to share their message of Christ allows him to mentor aspiring authors through a marketplace ministry.

Scott and Leah adore the Lord and the calling He's placed on their hearts for loving people. An experienced speaker and mentor, Scott remains amazed that God allows him to serve.

ALSO BY RICHARD BRIGHT


Love's Letters (A Collection of Timeless Relationship Advice from Today's Hottest Marriage Experts)

Really, Marriage Can Get Better: The 2 Small Steps That Can Bring Love Back to Life

Imperfect Dads, One Perfect Father: Encouraging Men Through the Journey of Fatherhood.

ALSO BY GEORGE GREGORY


Love's Letters (A Collection of Timeless Relationship Advice from Today's Hottest Marriage Experts)

Imperfect Dads, One Perfect Father: Encouraging Men Through the Journey of Fatherhood.

ALSO BY JUAN MARTINEZ


Beyond the Yellow Brick Road: Unlocking the Promises of God

Love's Letters (A Collection of Timeless Relationship Advice from Today's Hottest Marriage Experts)

Imperfect Dads, One Perfect Father: Encouraging Men Through the Journey of Fatherhood.

## ALSO BY SCOTT SILVERII

Favored Not Forgotten: Embrace the Season, Thrive in Obscurity, Activate Your Purpose

Unbreakable: From Past Pain To Future Glory

Retrain Your Brain - Using Biblical Meditation To Purify Toxic Thoughts

God Made Man - Discovering Your Purpose and Living an Intentional Life

Captive No More - Freedom From Your Past of Pain, Shame and Guilt

Broken and Blue: A Policeman's Guide To Health, Hope, and Healing

Life After Divorce: Finding Light In Life's Darkest Season

Police Organization and Culture: Navigating Law Enforcement in Today's Hostile Environment

The ABCs of Marriage: Devotional and Coloring Book

Love's Letters (A Collection of Timeless Relationship Advice from Today's Hottest Marriage Experts)

Imperfect Dads, One Perfect Father: Encouraging Men Through the Journey of Fatherhood.

**A First Responder Devotional**

40 Days to a Better Firefighter Marriage

40 Days to a Better Military Marriage

40 Days to a Better Corrections Officer Marriage

40 Days to a Better 911 Dispatcher Marriage

40 Days to a Better EMT Marriage

40 Days to a Better Police Marriage

# More titles from
# Five Stones Press

fivestonespress.org

CPSIA information can be obtained
at www.ICGtesting.com
Printed in the USA
LVHW081605170721
692830LV00002B/6